The Calling

*Love Knowing Moving,
Manifesting the Deep*

B Prior

First Published in 2019

BERNIE PRIOR FOUNDATION LTD

30 Teddington Rd, Governors Bay,
RD1 Lyttelton, New Zealand

Contents

Prologue

This book is a day by day collection of quotes, short pieces, conversations, pointers and awakening gems, from retreat journeys with B Prior in India, Tuscany and Crete during 2018.

Unique and complete in itself, every retreat is a timeless duration of Now, a chrysalis in which the true alchemy of life takes place. From sacred to profane, the themes, patterns, frequencies and colours that define the human experience and dilemma, appear and resolve in the open gaze of an expanding field of conscious Awareness.
As old ways dissolve, new life opens in pristine shapes of beauty. Above all, it is a 'return' to what one truly is, within and yet beyond the comings and goings of life.

The sessions are unscripted, conversational, unpredictable and permeated by the piercing purity of true Self-enquiry. B's words and presence, his fire, astuteness, humour and love re-ignite the flame of one's deepest calling within.

The writing is kept in line with B's verbal style to fully maintain the essence and transmission of his teaching.

Be silent and slow in reading. Pause often and allow the words, as much as the space between them, to reveal the mystery they are pointing to.

India Retreat

*"In any experience, go deeper than the relative.
Relate only to awakened Knowing."*

Rishikesh

Day One

*"You don't have to 'do' anything with your self-images.
There is the simplicity of seeing: "It is not I.""*

Give Your Power to Your Heart

'What I am' is Freedom itself. Life simply terribly,
awfully, wonderfully, magically manifests where I
move power or attention to.

Withdraw your attention, your power, from the body-
mind and give it to your heart and you will be your own
undoing. Isn't that wonderful!?

Awakening To The Depth Of What You Are

When you fully relax in this openness, the contracted
forms of your relatedness break open. You begin to be
in the experience of the illusions you put together to
relate to, in the belief you needed 'things' or needed to
be 'someone' to realise *What You Are*. See, that the
contraction is in everything you made, to experience
yourself as a self.

You have to really love awakening to the depth of *What
You Are,* because this level will fall apart to come back
together differently from the realisation. It is all made of
you. You only ever kissed yourself, you only ever saw

yourself, tasted yourself, argued with yourself, only ever loved yourself. It is *all* made of you; you who is aware, knowingly aware.

Our fear is that our Knowing knows that the illusion 'I am someone' will fall apart, but in the falling apart I realise the depth of What I Am. And the depth of What I Am realised or awakened to, becomes a functional movement all the way up to the surface. New forms form directly as What I Am, as aware Being formed. The unseen brings that into pure forms that will pass away and yet the light that form is made of will never pass away.

You are the Beingness that Sees And Knows

If you don't know yourself you will believe you are the 'self'. But you are The Self.

If you don't know yourself, you will think that all the habits, all the polarities, how *What You Are* put together a body-mind that you have identified with is 'you'.

If you don't know yourself, through being knowingly aware of yourself, you will think you *are* this self.

If you sit openly, watchful, patiently, you will see that you are not your self. You are the Beingness that sees and knows. Awareness knowing the Self and its development.

What it requires is *'you in it'*, totally. Let the subconscious come up into the light of Awareness,

which is you. Let it be felt. Let it go wherever it goes.
Wonderfully leave it alone but move in the deeper
knowledge not trying to escape any sense of feeling,
mental, emotional or psychological. Meet it as the light
of Awareness. No need for it to change or go away or
do anything.

It will resolve in you being Aware Knowing.

Immediate Verticality

Be deeply real about what the meaning of awakening is,
which is basically negating any need to reference the
past, any need to reference the future, which puts you in
immediate verticality. It is immediate.

Such a life opens your eyes.
Such a life opens your heart.
Such a life opens you to *You*,
prior to the belief you are 'someone'.

Day Two

*"Your life is a formation of what you give your power
to, imagination, thought and feeling or the depth of the
Real You."*

Mobile in the Deep

In giving your will to what is deeply calling you to *You*,
the return of your power through your heart, you find
that you are mobile, moving in the deep.

It's a movement. Sometimes it's swift, other times
gentled, sometimes a flow, deeper and deeper
nothingness opening. You know you are moving into
deeper *You*. You remember *You*, undivided, not held
back. In that moment, you are able to perceive form
formlessly.

All is Really Vertical

What I am pointing to is: all is really vertical.

The vertical is an outpouring of the unending deep,
which is the one who is listening to these words now.
That then lands in expression within the cosmos, for
you are a cosmic being, all the way into what appears to
be a horizontal plane of existence, but really the
horizontal is a vertical flowering and just like a flower,
it doesn't close when it closes, it just comes home.

Let the Horizontal Belong to the Vertical

The horizontal is the 'me'. It is horizontal. Simply make it belong to the vertical. Much to think about on the horizontal; past and future. Pay attention only to the vertical.

In Awareness, that is the one who is listening to these words now, you discover that *What You Are* is the ground of all that is.

It is like a fountain of *What You Are*, realising and expressing this 'I' that I Am.

This is what is, right here and now.

Beingness That Has Real Form

When you who is aware of Knowing realises that you know already as Knowing, what use is the mind in telling you anything?

The mind is of no use to you now. You don't need to know a flower, know another, know some 'thing' as if it were an extension of you. Suddenly it is all what you *are* as Awareness.

The belief in cause and effect is the belief that you are a 'someone' doing something. Then you have polarities, good and bad, right and wrong, happy and sad. *What You Are* is joy itself that needs nothing, just like when you were a child, not the name that someone gave you but the movement of Beingness that had real form. That form was not created out of a cause and effect, it was *You* as Being coming to the surface of what you are as Reality.

Your Subconscious Will Come Up

As you awaken to the depth of Knowing, you also land in the forms and appearances of your familiar likes and dislikes. They literally come up. Your subconscious comes up.

You will definitely experience this in the sensation of your body-mind, in the manner in which you have used thought and feeling to move by a thought or a feeling. All that will start to collapse for you, if you are genuinely awakening to what *You* first deeply *Are*.

In Knowing or in what is vertical then, simply bring what you thought was past and future into this moment of verticality. That means you deeply, deeply know more than how you constructed a sense of self. You deeply, deeply know that you are more than what your thoughts and feelings tell you.
Eventually you will realise that you are more than the universe that spilled out of your bright Awareness.

To stay vertical, when you keep wanting to 'lay down on the job', to bring what you thought had a past and a future and only respond to what your heart of Knowing is, takes a great love of what you deeply are. A love of what is beyond your believed experience that you're a body-mind and you must follow and conform to thoughts and feelings.

Our thoughts and feelings are expressed as the world, not the earth which is an expression of the heart, but the patterned levels that Awareness has covered the heart of Being with.

In awakening deeply, all your distractions will rise to the surface of your nervous system, of your body, your mind, your feeling sensation and within all your relationships. You will really be knowing yourself and you *have* to know yourself, because then you know that that self is *not* you. This is just the beginning of what you are as Awareness awakening to Pure Knowing, reforming the forms of this humanness; not through doing but through going deeper and moving as a being.

There will be much for you to contend with from the verticality. It is not that you can just leave this horizontal plane alone. It is that 'all this' is allowed to be in your Awareness direct, no matter how it feels.

Most of us move away from the opportunity this presents, which is the realisation of *What I* truly *Am*, the master of the mind, through belonging to what I deeply know in meaning within me, and the transformation of this reality which I am now filling out as Awareness, not as a somebody.

Dip a Little Deeper

Through your small self you will never be able to explain the Reality you are in an embodied way of depth. Yet you have form and this form is in a level of your bright Reality and *you* who is the One, is awakening *on* this level to inform this level of who I Am, this 'I' that is listening to these words now.

Not to inform the people! No, this whole level, to fill this level up with your bright Knowing: I Am That.

If you go a little deeper you come into a place where it is not that you are explaining, but you are *living* the realisation.

We must dip a little bit deeper than our usual manner of conveying what we are. If we look, our life is a conveyance of what we believe in. Your life is a formation of what you give your power to; imagination, thought and feeling or the depth of the Real You.

Your sense of mind and emotion, all these vehicles are that in which Awareness direct conveys what It is, without any movement of a sense of self or being anyone. That mind, emotion or feeling sense 'I Am' conveyed directly without any thought or need to construct feeling in any particular manner. Those are all constructs. This notion that I am 'someone', it's a construct. You are Pure You already, but now you see that in everybody and you see that you can merge!

Of course this is an intimacy beyond the current evolution of what we call mankind. But are you the

'kind' that can bring what You Are? That alone evolves
humanity for you are not a person, you are the whole of
humanity. That is what you are on this level and yet you
are beyond. This is a formed movement of You being
You. You can go to many other deeper levels and fill
out the level, but You are the seamless movement
beyond all spaces and times. That is the movement of
Love.

What happens 'here' is that the body-mind begins to
empty out of this constrictive idea that you are finite.
The only thing that is finite is this moment of forming
that passes away and is reformed immediately, at a
tremendous speed, registered in the nervous system, in
the body in the cells. You are the entirety of existence,
Now.

In our conversations in everyday life then, if we learn
not to bypass constriction, contraction and learn to
allow it totally and do our best to remain open, we
discover the contraction is not what we are, but a level
of the body-mind held in the belief 'I am someone'.

In any moment that we converse, that contraction points
us to what we are holding onto and it has such power
because that power holds the table to look like a table, a
flower to look like a flower, the universe to look like a
universe. That power holds the body together in a
shape, so that the shapeless can talk to 'itself' in shapes
of Love. You are holding your body together in a
particular modality of a person. When you awaken, you
discover that contraction and set it free of your
holding. We can come from a deeper place in how we

commune and communicate, but we must let go of this familiarity that I am someone and you're someone else.

Q: Is that the essence of the infinite?

B: You *are* the infinite. If you looked in the mirror, the seeing is you, not the image. The seeing and knowing is what You are, not the forming an image. That is all made of what You are.

As you move in this level of Reality, which is you, then this level will only form what You are *in it*. If you're not the freedom of your true nature, then you realise the forces that you are holding together, how you separate experiences into this, that, and the other.

Eventually you realise what that is, that separation is a 'doing' of you. When you go deeper, the separation will be known to you. That is knowing yourself. Knowing yourself is knowing how You-Awareness form this conditional level of you into forms.

When you arrive here, which is now, everything is possible, for you are the impossible made possible in every moment. And only you can raise the horizontal to the vertical by being deeply what you deeply are, by being true to what you know in your heart.

The Pressure of the Enormity You Are

In awakening you are far too much for this little body you call 'me'. You will be bursting at the seams, mentally emotionally, socially, in every way.

What you do as Awareness, is keep memory, which is power attentive to past belief. Thrown forward, you call that future and you control your energy and your power to manifest familiarity. Therefore you will not 'feel' in your sense of self under pressure, what is *deeper* than how you put that sense of self together.

When you were a small baby you did not have this. You were completely spilling out the radiance of no-thing, no body, no name, no bother and no care. You were care free. The moment you started to believe in a name, ascribed to a particular family group and society, you began to be under pressure, because of the enormity of what You Are with no beginning and end. You are contracting into a name, identified with particular people, who are also illusory, for there is only The Self.

Then you as Awareness, constantly stay true to the false, true to the imagination that you existed in the past and that you belong to a particular culture, a particular conformity. You didn't recognise it as conformity but you conformed to have a comfortable life for a self, an easy life but an illusory life for You are uncontainable. You stay true to the bonds, which are the chains of familiarity. Your body becomes familiar, everything becomes familiar whilst you actually know that there is no fullness in this, no Reality in this. It's like clockwork - round and round and round.

The moment you have a little bit of awakening, just a tiny bit is enough, the whole thing blows apart. The moment you begin to have awakening to what is deeper than your sense of self, this puts everything under pressure that you have put together as a sense of self. You, your love, your friends, your family, your society and this world is now about to break open for it is all *in You.*

Awakening puts your existence as a 'someone' under tremendous pressure because the power You are is immeasurable. You are infinite. You will go through what one realised man called 'the eye of the needle'. Through your own 'I' you will go. Everything that you believed was 'you' cannot get through. This is what you experience as you awaken to what you could call 'the other side', but it's not the other side, it's just the deep of that that I Am. You realise you are both sides, which have no sides.

You see, What I Am is dismantling you in your own interior, because you and I are the same one. This life undoes you to reveal You to You. Responding to the infinite invitation of being what you deeply are with every breath is simple, be honest and one with Knowing in everything.

What a Wonderful Life

It is not You that changes, only the forms spilling out of your changelessness change, in an attempt to give form to your infinite nature. This is why everything moves, because You have no beginning and end. What a wonderful, wonderful life discovering how deep I Am.

Day Three

*"Only You can raise the horizontal to the vertical,
by being what you deeply are,
by being true to what you
know in your heart. "*

Belonging to Being

Self-mastery only comes through belonging to Being
and listening to Being. Being is omnipresent, it fills all
things you could possibly ever taste, know or be 'subject
to'. But no subject is subject to anything for there is
only one subject and it is 'I', infinite aware Knowing and
within What I Am there are infinite realms of Being
possible to manifest in this level of reality.

No Such Reality

No one ever lived in the past, because there is no such
reality. No one will ever live in the future, because there
is no such reality.

In the full recognition of this, Freedom, which is
inherent in Being is lived, regardless of any images of
yesterday passing through mind.

A Universal Body of Pure Presence-ing

When you get clear that what you are is the deep,
Awareness knowing it knows, that straightens

everything. Its movement is a movement of Oneness in that Awareness true to Knowing, Pure Being or Love, moves up to the apparent body, and this body becomes a universal body of pure presence-ing. In such a vibratory field of such a living presence, cells within cells within cells begin to match that presence.

You may be walking down the street and you see someone turn, they see you and they think they know you but they know Thee, what you are coming into as the One within them, where there is no 'them and you' but only 'I'. It's a conveyance 24/7, never does it stop this conveying of what truly is. It's a shared experience.

This changes the very cells in your body, which actually changes the cells in the universe. The cells in the universe appear as stars, planets, as many different divine forms of Reality appearing. You might be clear that there is a star appearing in the sky, but it is actually the divine intellect, it is You appearing through the black, the forming of the Knowing of the movement of the light.

When one realises, more stars are discovered in this apparent formed universe. Stars are realised beings. You discover that inner movement isn't a movement of something physical, mental, psychological, it is a movement of Being. Then the phenomenon of the body is able to translate the movement of Being into physical moving expression: This!

Remain Open

To be truly sincerely deepening and awake, it doesn't
matter what kind of a 'What Is' appears. Remain open.
Remain open to convey and to be. Don't cover up.
Remain open, be Love. Don't revert back to thinking, to
mind, to limitation, to holding on. Stay genuine and
clear in what you are awakening in, no matter what
appears on the surface.

On Therapy

Q: *Could you comment on the meaningful-ness or lesser
meaningful-ness of therapy.*

B: It has a great deal of meaning, as long as one does
not have a self-image. If one does not portray a self-
image then the flow of what is imageless, the
conveyance of what is deeper, is possible.

When every image is dropped in our meeting of one
another, we are a movement and flow of Being and
anything is possible. Miracles are possible. The
rebuilding of the body-mind in a new code of Being is
possible. So is therapy meaningful?

Yes, as a stage of development and certainly in the
support of the body-mind in terms of supporting its
openness on the surface. It looks like we are giving
therapy or supporting 'somebody' but actually it is much
bigger. There is the support of the body of humanity,
which is the possibility of infinite Awareness opening
the gates of eternity. You *will* walk into the gates of

eternity when the body drops away and you *can* drop the body mind idea away, here and now.

Therapy coming from the imageless has a place until it is displaced by what is deeper and what is higher.

It is also dependent on the evolution of the beingness of one who appears to be somebody. Some need more support of what is imageless in the body-mind than apparent others. Some are able to have flow through them the self-transformation of the whole of humanity and others can just accept or deal with the transformation of a limited self.

It appears that everyone is in the same place but it differs according to your state of evolved Consciousness. The body will match that. The body that you appear to come into is on loan. You come into the right body for the body of Awareness to move through and be What It Is, which brings about self-transformation without a cause or effect.

Cause is an effect of so much more than what medicine thinks it is at this stage of evolution. Most medicine is bound by materialistic ideas of what a body is and who looks and speaks through this apparent body. That's changing, especially in those that are awakening. You will be in the more immediate experience of what is changing to become deeper than anything that can change.

Illness is not necessarily a disfunction, it can be what one has taken on in the psyche, but make no image of this, otherwise you will believe you are 'someone' doing this. Stay with the Beingness and be with Being when you relate. That is more than healing. That is moving in a deeper body of Being, having access to the beyond, moved into embodiment. It comes through.

The body-mind idea has you imagining you are a someone and limited but you are not. You have to go beyond that and there are moments when you must utterly dismiss the idea that you are an image. Sometimes, when you are dismissing the idea that you are an image, you come upon a wall or an old code within the psyche and within *your* psyche. You are not given this by another, you took it on. Not 'you' as a someone, but *You* as Awareness-Knowing. You come into this level of you to be all that *You Are* within this level and to fill it out with your radiance or your Knowing. This will change how you perceive 'What Is'. It will change you, you will relate totally differently.

Day Four

*"Realising is all there is. Awakening is all there is.
Whether you know it or not, what you're awakening to
is what you actually ARE.
It moves, it lives and it jumps from one cell to
another. It's impersonal, it's a dance, it's what you
love."*

A New Power Begins to Move

When you awaken and you still use thought or feeling
to deliver the message of Knowing, you still believe you
are 'someone', then you have to use a lot of energy to
stay there. You contract just to keep thought and feeling
matching your familiarity. It will all become too much
and at some point you are going to burst. Who knows
how life is going to help you burst; it might be a
breakup, a misfortune or an accident or you simply drop
this idea that you need to feel good to be what you *first*
Are.

You can just drop the lot and be Being Knowing,
moving. You will be knowing the peace that you are
without contriving the need to get peace, the love that
you are without the needing to feel love.

You will be Freedom itself, no matter what, because
that is the truth. New power begins to move through
your blood. The power of Love, the power of patience,
the power of presence, the power to give, give, give and
give. You are an endless ocean. The walls will break

and you drop into what You Are. Unbelievable, yet *now* you believe it.

Your Body is a Living Code

Your body, what appears to be the body, is as much the 'OM' as that symbol on the wall over there. This body is a living code of the direct realisation of 'I Am'.

I am not speaking about an idea of this physicality, that's a mental thing. Necessary as it is on this level, but it is a mental thing: a picture of the body has formed, but prior to the brain there is a body of Awareness that you move by, even in this body.

There is no death for one who realises this.
You can travel the universe in your real body, your body of Consciousness.

No End to Realising

There is no end to realising, whilst having an apparent physical form, that realising is a living Oneness all the way up into this human experience of Oneness.

So wherever this One moves, throughout the realms of its own Reality, filling up that level with *What You Are,* that realm transfigures, reforms and another life of Consciousness begins.

You have bridged the surface with the deep, you who is knowingly aware. Not with a thought but in the direct belief, 'I Am' and the opened experience of that within your own experience of Being.

On this level of reality you will see that for you everything in action or movement is different. The body moves differently, because as you move from the deeper awakening, you move encoding this level of reality differently. Everything here is upgraded, simply because of what you realised as Awareness. Your old life couldn't take such power.

Living Beings

Q: *I had the most beautiful meeting yesterday. I was very touched by the energy down by the river and then the river was flowing through me and I came home. It feels like everything has changed and shifted in me since then.*

B: The river is as much a being as you and I. The hills are a being, the pigeons are beings, everything is of Being. This river is a being and if you sat here for a while, you could converse with it in the deep, like you could with anybody here. You would need to resolve the distraction of believing you are a 'someone', to speak to such a being.

Realise, that the river realised you. Two rivers becoming one flow. You are a river. This is what you recognised, this is what cleansed you, this is what opened you to what you called 'home'. The recognition of two beings merging, the same river. It just looks like that one is out there, flowing down there but you are as

much a river as that river. You met in the river of Being.
Now that kind of meeting is sublime. Keep meeting that
in all that you meet. Here are rivers, *(points to the
people)* beautiful streaming rivers, not to be judged by
the colour of their skin, age, gender, culture; all flowing
rivers. Rivers realising rivers, realising rivers. It is the
return to the ocean of Awareness. Just a pointer on the
way to nowhere. You will give up the idea that you are
going somewhere, you are going nowhere and nowhere
is *What You Are*.

Day Five

"The moment you see yourself navigating through weather, close up the compass, turn off the GPS, be clear and true to Knowing."

Compassion

Your deeper yearning is for all beings to be free but will you allow pain in another without telling them anything? Will you allow that pain to be fully known? Will you *be* that pain?

Your pain is not that they are 'awakening but not living it'. Your pain is that you want every being to be free. It is a very beautiful pain and in that you will burn ever deeper.

Pain will literally turn into compassion. Compassion is you going right into the intimacy of another and what they are. That is compassion. In deeper levels we literally become each other. That will nourish your heart and the deep will open even more. It calls you to really come into this life as Being Knowing.

The Golden Thread of Knowing

There is need to check out the weather, no need to make believe that all is good. It is all just in the knowing of *What You Are*, which has no opposite. It doesn't mean having a good feeling, a good experience.

The One Good is here, listening to these words in any weather. That straightens up all the levels of the body-mind, you can feel it coming up the body and raising up the vibration. Belong to the smallest Knowing, which is the smallest thread and this thread is running throughout all life, this thread 'I Am'. Only the Real is on this thread. There *is* only the Real.

The illusion of the belief that I am a somebody and that I need to navigate through any weather, is not on this thread. The illusion that I need to feel good is not on this thread. But this thread is able to make all that you have in this life real. It is able to make it real by turning the Knowing of this life to whatever you do.

When you are doing something and you meet some 'weather', the weather of the mind doing this or that, the weather of thoughts and feelings, the weather of grief, of anger and of emotion, don't look for a destination and a way to get through this. There is none. *You* are not going anywhere.

When there is 'weather', which are the conditional sense-forms of you as a somebody, don't navigate through it to find some form of goodness, of rightness or of feeling. You give up your compass! The weather will get a little bit more turbulent but you are not navigating, you are being true through the heart. Then those pieces of weather, which are old habits and ways of functioning are transformed in the weather-less You, the light of You.

Wherever you are true in whatever you are doing, levels of the body-mind are transformed. They are like seeds

of Reality that then belong to the golden thread.
Integration in the body and in the mind. Integration
means, no weather can affect that level of You in your
self and person. Eventually the whole body-mind of the
self and person is integrated in the golden thread as
Knowing. All that you are and all that you have in the
body-mind is being tugged, it is like a hand pulling the
golden thread and no matter what weather you are in,
you know you know more than trying to navigate the
weather. This plane of reality will never cease having
all sorts of weather.

All Matter is Equal

The moment you come from just a little bit deeper than
the 'weather' (within and without), you're in the
beginning of *What You Are*, that has no end. In not
navigating the weather you then are that intelligence in
this human level of reality.

This is what makes humanity real and Reality real
humanness. The moment you see yourself navigating
through weather, close up the compass, turn off the
GPS, be clear and true to Knowing.

First what happens is a sense that everything can rest
and nothing matters, not in the old way of 'nothing
matters' but in the way that nothing really matters other
than this Knowing, which *makes* everything real. Then
the mind has no images of what matters more than any
other matter. Then all matter is equal. All matter is
equal, there is nothing that matters on its own. It *all*
matters, in other words it's no longer controlled by a

mental attitude and an emotional movement. Matter is illumed then by the light of Knowing. All is equal on every level.

This equilibrium is Pure Awareness knowing it knows. Nothing is singled out. Everything is the singular, the whole, nothing is divided. In that immediate Knowing: 'nothing is divided' you settle down, immediately in your humanness *as* this Knowing being human. Then *all* weather is glorious.

Undivided

On this level of reality, *Reality* or 'the Real' is the one who is listening to these words now. Not a self, not a body. Everything seen on this level of reality is made of the light of *Reality* itself. No subject and no object.

Objects then do not tell you or determine *What You Are*. They are instruments of the light of perception of *What You Are*: undivided attention, total *Reality* filling out this reality with You as Awareness.

The Wonder of the Deep Formed

Keep walking into the deep. Let the deep have your
legs, let the deep have your lungs, have your heart, let
the deep have your life! It is remaining truly present,
truly here and now.

Day Six

"All of life, regardless of how it looks,
conspires to directly show you,
you are already free."

Man and Woman

Q: Can you expand on the meeting of man and woman?
I hear you usually speak this…

B: I haven't spoken of this in aeons! Let's look at what
is *first*! Man and woman is what is *last*, they just keep
putting themselves first.

When you say: "I hear you speak of...", right there you
can enter a deeper frequency direct as Knowing. If you
are hearing, hearing is made of the Knowing. It looks
like you are hearing through a brain or through
somebody with experience, but hearing is made of the
Knowing, sight is made of the Knowing and taste is
made of the Knowing. All the elements are made of
Knowing. Prior to the elements 'I Am knowing I Am'.

Stay with that, then anything that someone over here
(B) seems to say that matches the heart of your
Knowing is not 'someone over here' knowing. It is
Knowing knowing and that is Oneness moving. The
field rises because the Knower-sphere is the Knowing
knowing it knows and everything rises up. That's the
transformation of self into a movement of Being.
It is essential for this to be *first*, otherwise we end up
putting what is last, first.

Man and woman do not come into this until the Beingness of what is man or the Beingness of what is woman is already entering this. The light of the Knowing and the light of Knowing being lived, being drunk, being walked, spoken, formed. This light of Knowing raises up an apparent man and an apparent woman. It raises up the Consciousness. Then there is man and woman, who are not actually man and woman. They are awakening on the level of Being, uniting Consciousness and Energy. When bright Consciousness and bright Energy get together you have the building of a Oneness relationship. You have a building of a union that is already taking place in the deep.

You have to be clear about this because that kind of connection is going to empty out this idea that you are a man or a woman. It will go right to the belief that you are a man that exists in time, a woman that exists in time. It will go right to that belief and undo the pockets of holding on to likes and dislikes, as a man or a woman. It will empty them.

Then you are called beyond this idea of man or woman, therefore you will go beyond the ideal of man and woman. That's an emptying out of a contracted belief that this has to look a certain conditioned way to work. Because if you made a connection in the deeper communion of Being, you already transcended the idea that you are man and woman. You met in the profundity of Being; Consciousness, Energy, brightness, already one. That's a state of Love but it's a Love that doesn't belong to a sense of self. It belongs to a movement of Being and the birth of the Being in every moment that is becoming. Never does it enter linear time. That's the mind's idea making an image of this meeting as a man and a woman. So there is this union of that that is already one. All the ideas of what it is to be a woman, all the ideas of what it is to be a man, all the ideas of what it is to be together are going to be a nice big funeral pyre!

Your old way is to get out of that fire. Your new way is to stay in it, because all that can burn is cause and effect. Images in the mind, imagination in the feeling sense, conditionality, that's all that can burn. It is burning away the condition to make way for the unconditional union, streaming from that place arriving in the heart, the body, the meeting, the right condition: emptiness. Emptied of the belief that I ever was a particular woman, a particular man. Then you are right here right now, infinite Awareness as woman, infinite Awareness as man.

The opportunity to realise the depth of such a meeting, without putting conditions on it and most definitely without control, is very rare, because the belonging to the knowing of Being and what it brings forth is your very love and if two can share that same knowledge and Knowing they can become one Love as one body, expressing the infinite nature of aware Knowing. They can mirror to each other in a living knowledge of what they are deeply entering, which is more than sense perception. They enter the mystery revealing the mystery.

Any name given to that, any plummet down is identification with linear time. You will need to go through that and not bail out of that or turn away from that invitation to clear that level through the burning of what you once believed in. But you are really seated in Knowing.

You have to be really deeply clear about this, because she will bring to him his nightmare of separation. She will bring it to him. She will lay it on his plate. She will bring all the forms that are causes and effects. You are given those for she has believed in those too. But if he has really seen her in the light of his bright Awareness and her inner dance of mystery, then she will empty out all causes and effects for she is none other than what he is as the Feminine Principle of a cosmic reality.

As Awareness, you need to meet the causes and effects in this body-mind, because they will spill out of him and they will show him what he loves. Does he love her in the depth of the Beingness that he knows he saw her in the light of his own Awareness or does he need something from her, want something from her?

If he is called to the light that he saw connected in his own heart, he will die for that and basically that's what happens.

And she will die for that meeting if she as aware Knowing has touched the depth of where he now comes from. She will practice staying open and self-emptying and it will cost her all her self-images, it will cost him all his self-images. Sometimes they want to get out of this, sometimes they will want to run and they will say: "I am out of here!" But really they don't want to be out of Here, infinite space, this Now, the eternal possibility of forming the relatedness from what is already one. That is their yearning, to know God in true forms of living loving Oneness. The mind will say: "This isn't working." but our heart will say: "Yes it is! It is absolutely working!" You cannot let go of such a love. It keeps calling you and calling you:" Die for me, die for me! Die for that that is true!" But it is never going to be for your self. It will be for the union point within, where energy and Consciousness move to the tune of realisers realising.

Day Seven

*"Awareness resolves it all. Nothing to solve. All
resolved in the being of aware Knowing."*

Space and Time

You do not move as space and time. Space is the infinite
nature of the One who really is Knowing. Time is the
truth that it has multidimensional outpourings,
unformed, unseen with the human eye but known in the
knowing of Awareness, pouring out manifesting what
appears to be a sense-perceptible universe. But the
universe is not made of 'sense', it only makes sense
here in your brain.

It is pretty unique in many ways, that the universe that
is just behind this, is a deeper reality outpouring in the
light of one's Knowing 'here' is made sense of. Never
does it move in time. It is a movement of Now, moved
by the deep, flowing like a river expressing what truly
is. It is not an appearance in a space of 3D dimensions,
but is an appearance in the space of infinite Awareness,
the one who is listening to these words now.

Your Own Social Media

The world is your own social media. It's in you, 'here'
this overlay of mind on the pristine no-image of the
earth. The earth is not an image, it's a living Beingness
moved by Goodness which is the One, giving the
possibility of expression in matter of true forms of

living Awareness. Then I can say: "I am That" and it doesn't just stay on the surface but the whole body responds to that living knowledge. Not a surface body, not an image in your mind but the openness of the real body, which is a body of Being. Being, prior to the image in the mirror.

Your body is not something fixed as an image, it's a sensation of Pure Awareness, a being that knows that it is Knowing, not a body but Knowing aware. It's direct, not anywhere else but right here.

Tiruvannamalai

Day Eight

*"She will lead you to Self-realisation
for that's what She loves. She loves
to lead you home to You,
for you are The Self and She is
already in your arms through your heart."*

You Are The Presence Of What is Here And Now

It is not that you are *stuck* in patterns, because you are eternal in nature. If you truly look, you will not know a beginning or end. Only if you as Awareness move in the ideas of the mind, you will wrongly perceive that there is a past and a future for you. But that's not the truth.

There is no past and future to you because you are the presence of what is here and now. These are not just words.

Now is the timeless truth of *What You Are* and there are moments when time doesn't exist, because unless you think in terms of 'horizontal', there *is* no time.

The Crumbling of The Belief in You as a Person

What you will go through and be meeting is the dissolution of ever believing that you were born, that you had past, that you will have future and that everything belonged to you as a person. All this will start to crumble. That's what awakening does! Only that that can crumble will crumble, everything else makes you truly wonderfully humble, truly wonderfully pure. You begin to realise *What You Are* and this will upset your plans for the future.

It is 'I' and it Appears as This Life

In being true I opened to Knowing and the Knowing appeared as my breath, the Knowing appeared as this movement that is ever present.

It is 'I' and it appears as this life and it is good. One can say 'it is good' and there is only the Good.

Then who is that that is speaking and knowing? It is the One that truly is. There is no one else here and it is 'I'.

No Power Over Presence

You draw to you what you have not yet understood is made of you. Dark or light, up or down, in or out, so then what the dark Feminine is, if you want to use that term, is the belief that there are past forms that determine what truly is. There is no such thing as a past form and no such thing as a power that has power over the presence.

Power belonging to a believed past with a believed future is the chaos that one may experience when one returns to the immediacy of knowing the Knowing as Awareness itself, displacing the idea of darkness in terms of past and future, want and need, this and that. That is all displaced, allowing Consciousness to realise what It is direct.

Integration is of 'Knowing', not of The Masculine and Feminine

Integration isn't of the Feminine and Masculine. It's the integration of Knowing. Knowing then moves in the Feminine and Masculine and then moves on the surface as a perceived man and woman. Men and women are not made of the Feminine and Masculine principles, they are made of Awareness, freeing Awareness from the polarity of any gender or 'agenda'. Otherwise you will not be free.

There is no Polarity In The Masculine and Feminine

Man: *In your teaching I have gathered that we're all Awareness coming into form and that sphere of the polarity of the Masculine and Feminine come into play.*

B: There is no polarity of the Masculine and Feminine. There's believed polarity when you have named yourself 'a man and a woman', giving the one who is hearing these words the possibility or the growing ability to manifest true conscious forms in appearance, in three-dimensional space and time, in you and everyone else, in a tree and in whatever you do, for *She* is not a woman. *She* is the profound energy and power, sometimes called Shakti, which is already one with the divine Consciousness, which makes all this possible and has a direction. The direction is the expression of Truth or the profound expression of Pure Awareness.

It takes a bit of enquiry to come into understanding the details of this. I will go first to Source and then 'downstream' so to speak. Sometimes if you ask a question, let's say about man and woman, I will go there but I will still take you back up that river. Otherwise Consciousness is divided between men and women and the idea of feminine power and masculine consciousness. You will keep dividing, but it is all within you. Give that a name, any name, and you are in duality. Stay with that in you and you will discover how *What You Are* is manifesting what you are belonging to in your Knower-sphere.

Man: *I can relate to that from experiences, this verticality of presence and the movement of attitudes or many different manifestations and forms taking place within and outside.*

B: Yes, but don't separate that for it's a singular movement. It is one movement and it never splits into two. Whether you say masculine or whether you say feminine, it is one total movement. If we could speak in the deep, which we can, we would no longer adhere to the law of manifest form. We would be in the law of metaphysical energy, Knowing and presence. The deeper you go a different law applies. So the law here, in what we are speaking of, is your possibility to manifest in a manner of Pure Knowing or pure control, which isn't control of somebody but it is You being so clear as to *What You Are*, that what pours into form is what you are being in another place.

Just like when you look at a baby, no matter what that baby is like, you don't see a distortion, you see a pure form of where that being is pouring from. There is nothing wrong there, it is perfect. When we add an identity to the one who is being and becoming, that is a polarity and distortion begins to happen. The moment there is anyone owning this in thought, feeling or any manner, there is duality. If you didn't add a name to *What You Are* the *What You Are* would simply continue to manifest in perfect forms of the immediate experience of what the deep is. This *is* what is present.

When You Fear Her, That is The Moment You Die For Her

Man: *Sometimes I have this joy, happiness and inner freedom and I recognise this in what you are speaking of. But when I am that joyful and happy towards a particular person, patterns come up fast, with woman in particular.*

When there is a beautiful woman and I am shining in my love and happiness towards her, she believes I want something from her or I have fear of rejection coming up.

B: You are demonstrating in how you speak of woman, that you believe she is other than another half of you, but she is undivided. You are dividing her and if you divide her you will fear her. You will speak in fear of her because you have divided her in you.

Behold her as you. Don't divide her from you because of the knowing that in beholding her you moved in self, to have her for your self, mistaking your self for You. You mistook your self for You. You wanted her because she is the other half of you. That calling is not division. You are calling her to you for she is the other half of you, but in your confusion that she is outside and separate from you, you call her for you in your self, where she is not one with you. Unless your self is made open like You, then to have woman for your self is to divide her from you. That shows up as 'you fearing her'.

What she is also demonstrating as *She* who has no name but is the tremendous beauty that you love as your very own self, what *She* is demonstrating to you, if you can see this is: in mistaking your self for You and having her for your self, you will have shame. Shame, that you took her for your self and divided her and made her two where really she is you, who is One. You will have guilt and shame on the level of person.

If you don't deal with that in terms of being true, clear and honest as a being, then that enters everyday life, in what you do, how you move, what you say and what you build. You will build something for you as a self, believing that's you as a being. You will even divide the manifest form of her, which will have you seeking her pleasure, her beauty, her profundity for your self. You will never find it whilst you believe that you will find her in and for your self but not directly in You.

Everything you do then will be for your self. Within that you are realising that the energy of what *She* is, is actually pure sexuality building the universe. Everything you do is made with her sexuality. If it is for your self it's sex, if it is for you as a being it is the manifestation of the making of Love. Whatever you do, whatever you touch, wherever you go is the manifestation of Love and *this* is what she loves.

You will know her in You. And in knowing her in you, she spills out in your self and she comes to you in form and she says to you "Never was I a body or a self, I am her, that that you love as You." And *She* makes form of her for you and yet she builds it in a sense of self, so that you can see her, hold her, be with her, kiss her.

What you are really kissing is the universe and bigger. If you love her that dearly, *She* will show you her cosmic body. You must be prepared to die to your self to realise her in you.

Then there is fulfilment and she will calm your heart and still your mind. First *She* will steal it and then *She* will still it; silence. You will begin to perceive so profoundly and deeply, you will weep that *She* could ever come into your arms.

Realise in you, *She* will lead you to Self-realisation for that's what she loves. *She* loves to lead you home to You, for you are The Self and she is already in your arms through your heart. This is what she loves: You being You, realised as your Self in your self. She dances for You, who is One with no beginning and end. *She* will take all your fear from you and show you the great Love *She* already is in you, as 'Here', but *in You*. Never were you two. When you fear her, that is precisely the moment you die for her...

You die for her by seeing her with your heart and knowing her with your heart, even though she crucifies you in your self. Then she will give you all her power, which is the power to manifest *What You Are* because you no longer need it. In this you serve all beings to realise the same, in You. That is Love without Duality.

Your love of her needs to be profound. To be profound you will need to go to a ground beyond your sense of self. She will ensure this is what you do and until you do, she will divide her from you, but this is her game. Did I answer your question?

Man: *Yes and way beyond! I have a belief that everything is Love and that's the most important in the whole universe.*

B: Ok, then keep that in Knowing. A belief that is real is not of your mind, it's not a thought. It is beyond your mind as a self. This is in the place of You, that I call 'You-Awareness'.

Man*: I sometimes feel this 'trying', you know, 'trying to be in love' and then not being true. There is a fear of being love, a fear to love and be loved.*

B: What does that have to do with woman?

Man: *It just 'shows' with women.*

B: Notice you said 'women'. Women are multiple, *She* is one. Let's stay with what you first said. You see her through many different sexual bodies. While you see her through your sense of self, she means more to you as sex rather than as Love.

Sex means: 'I need more experience of her sexual body, before I can commit to love her'. That's duality. That means that you are confused, on a real level you're confused. You are believing that what you love is the body of woman but not the love of *Her*, which is her real body.

So you put faces and bodies on her as if her face and her body is *Her* and it's not. *She* shines free of any face or any body. That's what *She* is; Love itself shining behind any face and any body.

Whilst you believe that you can experience *Her* in many different women, you will be using your self and what *She* is, related to your self. It will turn her into a movement of sex. You are needing more sexual experience before you are available to no longer need sexual experience to be what *She* is.

You will go through woman after woman after woman to see that you are totally dissatisfied but you have not met *Her* as yet. You might have had a lot of sex and in the tantra field you might have had 'great sex', but great sex is not immense Love. So then the sexual energy is still only forming a self-identity. Then what *She* is cannot form what your heart is because you are needing more sex.

Until you give her up in wanting experience rather than meeting what *She* is, *She* can only display herself in a multitude of bodies that you chase after and never become settled with. You will need one tantric session after another, and will go from one experience to another and this shows up in all your life. You will need this experience and when that project is done you will need another experience...This is how it works.

Finally, you are called only to be one with her in Love, then you're going to be called to go through the eye of a needle, where all your past activity and your past sexuality is met to burn up the belief that *She* is a body and *She* is sex. *She* is Love! You will go through hell then, more than likely with a woman, to meet what Love is and die through the idea that she is sex.

Her Love forms the relationship of where you are coming from and what she opens herself to, in you. Her lower endeavour is to hold on to you, to hold on to your consciousness at a level that she wants to shape in her old known way.

Then finally you meet someone who is drawn to more than having sex and more than to holding a relationship through not allowing anything to change. Then there is a possibility that you will go through the loop together into the realising the One, transforming sex from lower sphere to radiant wholeness. Transforming the consciousness in a direction that brings you both into Self-realisation and bliss.

Then forming Love, moving Love, the realising of more Love is the energy, body and consciousness that you begin to move by. It just keeps deepening. All the old images pull out of your mind, your root chakra and everywhere. No longer is sex distorted as something for you, but it opens as that that transports Pure Consciousness into depth of great possibility of embodiment. Great Love begins to have pure functionality in a relatedness that is non-dual. Non-dual means that there is nothing to fight over anymore, no duel, no need to fight as two but to move in the Oneness. You realise, because you die for this realising. The fear is the need to have further experience rather than profound awakening, which ends all need of experience. You *are* That. Only in that manner can tantra bring Self-realisation for both, the apparent man and woman. Then it is an embodiment and a relatedness that is not two but one.

To believe you still need further experience of more women, is to live in the past. You have actually gone beyond that but your mind tells you that you haven't. Head upstream to where *She* really is. *She* awaits you. All your fears then will be let loose, realise they are false evidence appearing real - using the energy of fear to propel you deeper, not in need but in the desire to realise what *She* is.

Day Nine

*"It's not that you will come into Freedom,
it's that you ARE Freedom.
A drop of water doesn't get lost in a puddle,
a river, in an ocean or in a cloud,
it remains water."*

This Instant

The light of the Self is simply that that is pouring out of
the profound black, which is Awareness, the Absolute.
That light seemingly has particles but is non-separate
and non-dual and is the first instant, which is also a
ridiculous thing to say for there *is only* the first instant
and it is *this* instant. There is no other instant. *This* is
the instant in which everything becomes instant.

This particle of Knowing can be said to be Being or
beings but all beings spring from the Absolute, which is
Awareness. Any cell in your body represents the whole
body, any particle of light represents light or Knowing
or The Self. Dependent on how one is knowing light in
a particle, also the whole realises 'What Is'. Then 'What
Is' is contained in that particle, but it is also the whole.
The part is the whole and the whole is the part.

The World is in You

The world is in you, not outside. If anything happens in
the world, it happens in the world in *You*. It does not

happen outside and if the world gets stronger, that is
you feeding the world your belief in duality stronger.

No Centre

When you are really *You*, you have no centre, you are
the movement of the entirety. You assume that your
sense of self is your centre, but no, your centre is the
knowing of the Knowing of any centre. Whether it's a
personal centre, a self-centre, a body centre, a thought
centre, a feeling centre, *You* are the centre of it all. Go
deeper and You are It; no centre.

The Only Experience

When you fully come into this level as Awareness from
the deeper knowing or your being, you might call that
The Self. When you have had enough of personalising
experience, then the only experience is Pure Awareness
knowing it knows, from which a seeming subject called
'I' and objects in apparent space and time manifest; all
within your own Awareness. It becomes clearer and
clearer that what you believe in on this level manifests,
no matter what it is. You can have what you want until
you realise You are all that truly is. Then what need of
want, what want of need is there?

No Longer Becoming

Look at the words you use. You believe words are just
words but they are the sound of You creating You.

Once you have become, you will be lost in becoming.
You will have to be lost in the becoming for some while
and you will become 'someone'. You have become.
Now realise you're over becoming! Realising is no
longer becoming anything or anyone. It is the undoing
of becoming anything.

Contraction is a Gift

Contraction is simply another pair of much lighter
hands holding 'What Is', pointing to a door on the
surface that leads beyond the surface into deeper
Knowing. Contraction then is a gift that should not be
shunned away. Contraction is calling your attention to
portholes into a deeper reality that as yet you can't see
or you refuse to go into.

A Taste

Bring all your attention directly to the Awareness of
Knowing, much deeper than your usual kind of
awareness on this level identified with thought-forms.
Know Knowing direct, not a thought. That is a taste but
that one taste is the whole.

One cell in the body is the whole body, one human
being is the whole humanity, one star in the sky is the
whole universe, one word is every word yet to be
spoken or spoken.

You delight in this. The delight is you delighting in you.
You will be extracting all the old forms. This will be too

abstract for your usual mind, the mind will get bored with this. You will believe it is *you* getting bored with this and you will pick up the known. If you pick up the known, see it in your hands and see it, like you never have before, it will become the new. It is you seeing from where you see from that that makes everything new. You are its power. It's made of the Seeing and the Knowing. Never did you become anything. The becoming is the miracle of You being you.

Is a taste ever lost? What is the taste of water? Is this some kind of other water? Does water have a past and future? You know it doesn't. Every taste is the first taste. How can there be anything else you're tasting? That taste is beyond a first or last taste, it is the *only* taste.

Keep moving as that first taste. You have not lost it but it will cost you the belief that there is anything to taste. This ends time in you. How can you go forward when you know you've tasted all there is to taste? How can you make distance of time of that first one and only taste? That's what you thirst for, the first one and only taste, for there is no other taste that tastes like that. You know this because you *are* this.

Here It Has Form

When you are emptied of the thought-forms of a particular stationary self, then that emptiness is now available to be filled by what you are awakening to. You grow in the Knowing of what you're entering. Here

this has form but it's all made of You knowing more of
You-Aware.

The Puzzle is Resolving

Q: *The words you speak…. they open something inside
of me and my heart just cracks open and there is this
pouring out of pain but it is so beautiful at the same
time. It really doesn't make sense, it's like a divine
puzzle.*

B: But now you're not puzzled. The pouring out is the
direct realisation of what you once were puzzled about
but now the puzzle is resolving. You're no longer
putting puzzles together. Now you are the well of
Being pouring, forming, moving, deepening, undoing,
returning, realising, expressing for all eternity, which
knows no beginning to end; and yet you are beyond
even that.

Everything is Seamless

There are no levels in You, there are no seams in You.
You move in: 'everything is seamless', all made of You.
Then you realise, 'I have no need to move, to realise
What I Am.' Then, that that one is streams, endlessly.

Day Ten

*"Forms that manifest from your being you cannot miss
because you are made of them, they are made of you;
it's a singular movement. Mind stands still for such a
movement of Being forming."*

Slowness in the Dance of The Form Reality Practice*

Doership is created when Awareness believes it owns
forms, thought forms, feeling forms, psychological
forms. Forms as others, forms as places, forms as the
past and believed forms in the future. When we own
forms, everything is quite speedy but they are all
thought-forms really, forms that don't have transparency
in them, denser forms.

When you dance *The Form* and you are in the
enjoyment of the slow movement that is the discovery
of: "What does form contain, what does a movement
contain?" and more precisely "What do 'I' contain?"
You discover a finer perception of form and the deeper
level you are entering. Everything slows down in your
perception when You who is aware are looking for
something finer. You will see directly as Knowing.
You're not looking for an object, you're looking for a
finer light-form of You.

You are entering greater depth of perception and a
greater depth of Knowing and within that you
apprehend a greater depth of intelligence and of Being.
The sweetness then is Beingness being revealed. It is
beyond your mind. You're extracting the more solid

forms of thought, psychological, mental and physical past. You're extracting the solid form called 'your name'. When you have extracted this level of your name you will go deeper and as you go deeper time stands still, because there is no time in that depth. Everything slows down in your perception. One drop of what you are entering, should it enter time, could be like a million years.

The sweetness is you getting in touch with your being. Its forms are sweet because you don't pass away. Mental forms, emotion, physical forms pass away but the forms of your being do not. When you're knowing the sweetness of your being, which is a greater depth of *What You Are*, this can stream up onto this level and through You being one with It, I call this Awareness-Knowing, that level begins to come into form.

You will no longer be interested in any construct of form, although its foundation will be in Being and could be said to be eternal, but the building itself, the building blocks, the size, the shape will be of no concern to you anymore. You will belong to where it has come from. That's the sweetness you are coming into, deeper levels of your own being.

Forms that belong to your person you hold together with power, given away to personal relationship. You whizz through them and there is no depth. You are just holding forms together and say that's 'mine' or that's 'me'.

Forms that manifest from your being you cannot miss because you are made of them, they are made of You. It is a singular movement. Mind stands still for such a movement of Being forming.

Time stands still because it's not made of time, not made of a person. That's the idea within temples, it's also the truth of the body, the body *is* the temple really. It is that in temples of such profound embodiment time recognises that it flows out of that timelessly, so it stands still.

Walking into such depth undoes the shallow appearances that cannot hold what you're coming into. The old foundation of your old way and manner is not sound enough, it can't take that power. How you use mind, how you move will, how you do, how you see and where from, all changes because it comes into a greater ground and all you do from that greater ground has stability in that that doesn't pass away.

When your mind belongs to your heart, which belongs to your being, which belongs to the deep, you are stable in the movement of mind because that stability has gone all the way into the depth of the sweetness you are discovering. That is actually what *The Form* is about. *The Form* is not you doing something 'over there'. *The Form* is your daily life. Come into a greater depth and your movement is the movement of that depth, formed living movement of Being.

*B is the originator of *The Form Reality Practice*, a five-part movement sequence, taught on retreats with B and by teachers world-wide. The Form, is the manifest vehicle to integrate and embody everything B points to.

Day Eleven

*"There is no non-duality or duality,
there only is 'What Is',
filling up all dimensions, outpouring all dimensions
and of itself dimensionless, whole.
That is what is here, and the listener is That."*

Pure Knowing

In Awakening you are entering into greater depth of
What You Are and it has no 'I'. That's why there is only
Knowing knowing. It is not known or knowable as a
subject with objects as it is on this level. It is Pure
Knowing. Moving as Pure Knowing you return as a
child, sweet, innocent and you move and it's all very
spontaneous but even that word doesn't mean anything
to you now, because it is just what You are. You are
already the movement that moves the stars and it is
'What Is'.

Infinite Possibility - Right Here Right Now

When you are awakening at a deeper level you can only
know it as Pure Knowing and you will just say "I
know!" and you're knowing it as Awareness, infinite.
Then there is infinite possibility within the Knowing
right here, right now in what appears to be someone's
life.

You are the Beauty of the Present

You are looking at beauty in the past but You Are the beauty of the present. When you are looking at something that you liked in the past that's your self looking at it and getting a feed. Your brain is flickering pictures and images of what you have programmed your mind to believe you need. It looks like people and places, but it is mostly mental and emotional attitude, wrapped in many colours. In deeper levels of your being none of this happens; all there is, is Pure Being.

Realisation is Now

Realisation is now. There is no one who is not a realiser realising. If you want to realise and keep realising states of formation and personalising experience, then that's what you're doing, but you are still a realiser realising.

The New Never Touches the Old

The new never touches the old, never. Never does the *new*, which is the deep, ever have any relationship to the old. *You* do. You're able to split Reality, you're able to move at an untold speed into the past and live it and you're able to live the deeper sense. You are the seamlessness.

Your mind thinks you can mix the levels but no, the *new* never ever touches the past. It is You that brings it all together. You are the seamless fluid that makes it seem like the new, the deeper realisation is mixing with the old.

Slowly, as you really belong to deeper awakening, you unmix. You begin to know you are un-mixing because although you can still reflect off of the past, it no longer touches you. There is no relating here because your relatedness is in the now, far deeper and you are integrating deeper levels of 'Being Now'. Those deeper levels of 'Being Now' never enter space and time in the manner in which you think they do, mixing with past ideas. That mixing is only going on in your mind.

Here and Now is Infinite

'Here' for is infinite. We say 'here' and the usual interpretation of 'here' is a place in which 'I' a centre' seems to exist, now.

'Here', the mind interprets as where a centre is here, a centre that has a knowing of form and yet never sees its face. A centre, in which the mind says, there is space and distance between the objects of Knowing.

Here Knowing is objective, I am knowing someone in their object-form and I am knowing some thing as an object-form. Whether it is a mountain, a tree, an animal, I am knowing an object. I never look at my body as an object. Why?

Because my knowing of Knowing-Being-Aware does not objectify my existence. I Am the centre of it. Therefore my body is not an object, it has become me. How come no other body is you? Why do you make another body an object? You don't make an object of your body, but it is. It is pretty amazing if you can see that...

Here the mind objectifies existence as an 'outside' but doesn't objectify 'my body', which is an object in my awareness. It then makes time, space, duration, distance, past and future, but 'here' is the infinite, no centre. Now is the truth that I, who am aware, can move right now beyond the appearance of this space time into deeper dimensions of Knowing, unformed.

'Now' is interpreted by the mind as time but 'now' is Awareness-Knowing able to move deeper than this moment that appears to be formed as a subject with objects. Now then is not time but infinity, eternity where the infinity (Awareness) can move in eternity into its body of Awareness, called The Self, multidimensional in nature. It is your brain that puts you in this particular place of here and now, but you can walk in deeper levels of now, and you do. You go and collect a deeper level in awakening and you bring it here. That's your inspiration. Then you attach that inspiration to being somebody and belonging to somebody and that limits you once again. When humanity moves as one, through realising, this will all be different but in truth the kind of intimacy which will be here then is already here now. It is thought, that makes this dimension seem so impossibly dense.

All is Made of Awareness-Knowing

'Equally', in the manner I am using it here, means everything is made of Awareness-Knowing. It is all equal. Equanimity is the truth that all you could ever smell, touch, know or move is made of Awareness-Knowing, the light in which we see, in which we know and taste. It is *all* made of light and that light is Knowing. And all that light knows is: 'it knows it knows'. It knows it knows it is aware. That is your primal experience.

Then out of this, without moving away from it, Awareness through Knowing streams pure realms of Being, and realms of Being that are conditional. Now Awareness is awakening in the realms of its Being. Awareness is awakening in its Self, the true Self.

This body-mind-self is just a formed mirror of the Self. This is not your self. Your self is Knowing! You knowing yourself manifests, the knowing of that Self in goodness, clarity, beauty. Knowing *is* your Self, You Awareness. You are not 'someone'. You are the centre of it all, wherever you go. Go deeper and you lose your centre. You won't need one the deeper you go. Every level you touch is You. There beings merge and pass through each other, very little difference in each other just enough to be Knowing-Being together, and that is beauty.

To the Beginning

You can travel to the beginning of time right now. You will not be bothered with much anymore. You will come into the timeless spheres of your being, where nothing is quantified. It is too vast to quantify it. That is what you love.

A Star in the Sky of Awareness

Q: *I really enjoy what you're pointing to, about equanimity and that we are all 'realisers realising' and there is no hierarchy of Knowing or knowledge. We're all at a level in a sense...*

B: What there is though, is the activation of the Knowing and building of the Knowing in Awareness, appearing to be somebody, which means that another being can be on a deeper dimension still wearing human flesh. It doesn't mean they are any higher or any deeper, it just means they are coming from a deeper place of reality than someone else apparently is. There is no distinction between 'other' in that place. But you are a being and you can be whatever you want to be or you can be what you deeply are. There is still no hierarchy but there are deeper levels of Being activated, appearing to be human. A star for instance, a star is a light of a profound being shining from a deeper place of essence.

'Whoever this is' will at some point beam in the sky of Awareness for Awareness is a sky. Everything that appears in it is a manifestation of the movement of Being-Aware. So, as you realise the light of *What You Are*, you will shine in your own sky. Here that will appear as a star. Some professor or other will go: "I have just found another star!". But it is You shining.

Pour Yourself Into All That You Meet

How can you love, how can you know 'What Is', how can you understand experience if you don't pour yourself into all that you meet? Pour yourself into all that you meet and you will understand what you've poured yourself into. The pouring of You is what you already are, free. That kind of freedom poured into another awakens their own original freedom. But nobody is doing it. So yes, I am very clear about pouring What I Am into these meetings, into walking down the street, into being where I am. I am very clear that that is Awareness awakening to its own Knowing.

It just seems like it is 'here' but then I can see how it plays and opens up as individual beings moving and how some beings have mixed themselves up with the mental, emotional attitude of fixed time-space. Nonetheless, we are all 'That' planted in what appears to be form. We are actually the field as well as the seed as well as the planter as well as that that reaps that. That's what we are. The idea is to raise up in the garden of this

life, what you are now realising in deeper Knowing.
Form any seed here of the possibility to match what is
vertical, is for you to *be* the verticality in what seems to
be a ground of mental and emotional form. It is not, it is
all planted in your ground of Being, which is prior to
forming. Then what is planted 'here', a human being all
wrapped up as 'being someone' cannot grow itself. It
needs to be watered by that that actually planted it. To
mistake yourself as a human being means you can't
grow *What You Are* in your humanity.

The tendency is to be 'human' and humans mostly relate
to the past and the need for a future, and positive and
negative vibes. They think they can raise themselves up
but they can't, so they stay in the belief, hoping things
will get better and then coping with what's actually
happening.

Q: *I am devising all these strategies....*

B: Totally. Then if you think you are human and all this
is happening because you are human, you build more
distortion. Distortion not as 'wrong', but you build more
distorted forms that you will relate to. You don't see that
you are aware, knowingly aware and it is that, as *You*,
as Awareness, that has planted this humanness. Like the
baby, no 'I centre', no centre. Loving experience, it's
pouring What It Is into this level. The 'I' then becomes
the seed in the ground of a greater reality, having form
as human.

In everyday life when you awaken, you water your
humanity with self-knowledge, relating to the heart.
That's watering your humanity. Then your humanity

grows through you being true to Knowing. Otherwise
you will just think this is endless repetition, which it is
if you're using the mind. The experience of being
human will be limited for you. You will stay in the
limitation of your father, your mother, your nation and
your religion, all limited because it passes away. But
you are the unlimited Knowing that planted the seeds of
a greater reality. Now reap them, that's the whole point.

To know deeper than personalised experience, is to
water your humanity and grow the seeds of a greater
reality, a deeper place of Knowing. You grow and what
comes from you is nameless and formless but tangibly
real. You convey a tangibly real reality beyond sense
perception and it begins to make sense.

No Distance and No Duration

You are moving at an impossible speed of 'now'. When
you awaken, you awaken to true knowledge which
cannot be captured in a time space, because it is now.
You become acutely deeply and gently aware of 'What
Is' and you're able to decode or read every level, prior
to it coming here.

Somehow this movement that we call life is integrating
so much more than a separate sensed life. Truly stars
are being integrated in a human life. Scientists have
already discovered that there is star-stuff in our bodies
and in the earth, but they put distance on it. It is said
that all this came out of a massive explosion that
happened X amounts of years ago, but actually it is an
expression that is vibrating now and it is 'sensation'. All

this is happening 'now', it doesn't have any distance and has no duration. It's all 'now'.

You Want to Meet You Directly

You want to meet *You*, in everyone you meet. Whether it's a tree, a star in the sky, you want to meet that directly in the level of form. You want to know what the formless is purely like in form.

A Movement of What I Am

There is this Knowingness in What I Am, this 'I' that is listening to these words now, that I am always more than what I do. What I Am comes before what I do, in fact What I Am moves what I do and there is no one that acts that. And so even the movement of the tree there in the wind, is a movement of What I Am.

That strikes in one, if it does, that all movement is profound and not limited to sense perception or a particular way of sensing or perceiving. In fact, movement is beyond what can be perceived but will flow into perception.

Infinity Moving as Eternity

Go deeper than just sense perception and the experience is of dissolving. I simply descend into the depth of What I Am, but I will always be aware, knowingly aware as aware Knowing it knows.

What I Am is infinite without beginning and end. In awakening we often touch upon this infinite-ness. This moment is infinite and *I am* the infinity. Somehow, without going anywhere, What I Am pours out into Now; the appearance or the movement of infinity moving as eternity. It is infinite in nature but no matter how I perceive, I am only able to perceive this level of infinity in form. I may experience it as conditionality but the conditionality is made of infinity appearing to be conditional.

Flower of Flowers

As you live this life attuned to the heart of Knowing, do you love your heart enough to give up your mind as a way, so that your heart becomes the only way? This is what happens when we awaken, we have more orientation and direction with each breath from the heart. The heart is the flower of flowers. You respond and a particular petal of that flower opens. You respond totally to *What You Are* beyond this flower and the root of it will flower the whole flower. That would be Self-realisation right up into the 'most high', right up into the 'most deep'. You would realise you are the entire cosmos, you as Awareness-Knowing and you are the Knowing of that cosmos, its supreme intelligence. You as Awareness-Knowing.

When we live our lives for this, instead of building a separate sense of self, we build a self that is one with the 'most high'. In any moment that you are true to Knowing as Awareness to your heart and deeper, a petal

on the flower of your real heart flowers, which flowers
a higher state of knowing Being. There is a flowering or
a nurture of the heart that opens up that that is beyond
the body, for the body is only an appearance in the
awareness of your Knowing.

By the wonderful love that one is and the genius that
spills out of that pure mind, a brain that is a divine
instrument, moves the Knowing into perceptions of
forming. So when you are true to your heart, you are on
'the return' and that heart level streams up and streams
down, deeper embodiment beyond a sense of a body,
but a body of Pure Consciousness in the living flesh.

When you live in harmony with what the heart is, you
go to the 'most high' and 'most deep' within, and the
within is quite clearly seen to already be flowering
everywhere. You see into the mystery because all there
is, is the mystery flowering. It is most delightful. It is
the delight of Being, it is that that you're looking for,
because you *are* it.

A Mental Location

Whilst you use thought, through the belief you are
somebody that has a particular life-stream to do with
thought, feeling and location, then this location is
actually a location of mentality. It's a mental
location. When you are moving life believing that you
are somebody, all that you can use is mind, the
patterned sense of self that is handed down since time
began. Then you're not actually You moving, you're a

puppet of personalisation of experience since time
began. But when did time begin please?
Now only.

Awareness Knowing Depth

You know depth, you are knowing it, Awareness is
knowing depth. No movement of mind, no movement of
anything. It is Knowing and you *are* the Knowing. Then
there is a bird singing made of deep Knowing-Aware
and the pillow case is deep Knowing-Aware and the
warmth in the bed is deep Knowing-Aware.

You have not moved out of the deep and yet it is
beginning to have lightness of movement and form. Not
just physical form, but a fineness of form made of the
light of Knowing. It has movement in that Awareness-
Knowing streams from the deep without leaving the
deep and all is silent, open.

There are no words for this, words are just pointers. All
is good as within one's depth of Awareness, Awareness
is streaming up from the deep *as* the deep. From light
the first Knowing-form: The Self.

That movement continues to open all the way up to
what could be said to be surface form. Everything is
made of the deep, whether it is sound, form, taste,
touch, it is all the deep and you have not gone
anywhere.

Love is Awareness True to Knowing

Love is the movement of Awareness being absolutely
true to Knowing. That movement is Love. It is not
union, that's just another idea. It is just 'What Is'.
Awareness being true to the light of Knowing. It is not
split into forms, objects or even into 'someone
knowing'. Knowing is Knowing-Aware. That's a
movement of profundity.

What Was Black Became White

Q: *Would you say that form and emptiness is the same?*

B: Without speed or distance one is the depth of Pure
Awareness. Silence *is* that depth because the truth is
that there is no thing, no one. It is all pure emptiness
which is the absolute Awareness. From that, Awareness
desired to know it is aware. Light streamed from
nowhere, filling up the perception and what was black
became white.

Q: *Time comes from that?*

B: Time is an invention of this level of intelligence not
as yet integrated into one's timeless nature. It takes not
only a change of mind but the surrendering of the
content of mind. In Pure Consciousness, the vastness
that is aware, there is only 'I' and deeper, I am not.
I am and I am not.

One and Zero

For What I Am to look into this deeply, everything returns to no-thing. And no-thing knows Awareness in all the shapes of things. Every single speck of the cosmos is known by and as Awareness knowing Knowing. Not objectifying. When an apparent one comes into this realisation you can read the cosmos like you can read this room, for it comes out of *What You Are*. Whether you call that silence or depth, it doesn't matter and yet *matter* happens on this level.

This, is a level of reality but there is a greater reality than this level of reality, *Reality* being the Self-radiance. Deeper levels than this do not change the level of Being. Being-Knowing-Aware, aware to Knowing, which is Being. The unchangeable is realised to be present here. Never has it gone anywhere. 'Here' is the experiment of bringing the unchangeable into changeable spheres.

No purpose, other than to realise what one is (if we take the 'n' and the 'e' off 'one', you are 'O': zero) The one is the moment of Knowing, the zero is Pure Awareness. So, when you are Knowing you become One and that one is the 'Only One'. Never are there others. And that One is able to go back through the zero and remain Knowing-Aware; the Absolute.

Be Deeper Truth

You are already Truth, you are already Love but for that movement, which is Awareness being true to Knowing, to flow up to this level as Love, you need to know yourself and *be* the deeper truth *in* your sense of self. That's being true to your heart. Then your self opens up and is immediately emptied and filled in the same moment. This is the immediacy of embodiment.

Care for Yourself

You want to come into what you truly are? Then care for yourself by loving what you know deeper. And when the self undoes, which it will, love the way in which it undoes. Understand yourself. It is not You. You are the Knowing.

Integration

As we awaken deeper, all the emptying out of the old way enables the deep way to manifest as a movement of Love. That is integration. So that the smallest thing you are doing is moved by a profounder place in Being. Whatever you are doing begins to be a movement that is from the deep. A real power that truly serves all beings.

Day Twelve

*"Open until you see, open until
there are no more blinds, open until there are no more
shutters down. Open all the way."*

Fascination With the Deep

When the fascination of the deeper calling within is
what you really belong to, you begin to understand the
unwinding of the self centre. Mentally emotionally,
socially, psychologically and in many other ways, it all
begins to reveal.

You can develop a keenness of Seeing and Knowing, so
that you are so keenly fascinated with the deeper
realising that you are no longer fooled by an old way
calling you to remember it in thought and in feeling.

Even this 'I-thought' is prior to the body. This 'I Am-
thought' is what the body is made of but never does the
I Am become a body. It is the entire cosmos. There is so
much more to what one is, but how to discover this
alchemy up on the surface?

Being fascinated by a little deeper than your old way
awakens the profoundly Real in you.

There is a sweet, sweet pull to what is profoundly real
in you. Whilst one has a body that level streams up to
the surface. Alchemy is daily life. Everything that
comes, no matter how it looks to the mind, is alchemy,
is transformation. Transformation doesn't mean

anything needs to 'happen', it simply means the Awareness that once thought it was a body-mind is now fascinated with the greater depth of what is available to it. It is realising What It is.

This streams up a new body-mind, it changes it. Then the Seeing and Knowing begins to be so immeasurably deep that life on the seeming surface begins to match the Knowing. It becomes a 'living Knowing formed'. Such a body, such a form you don't leave behind, because it is the body of realisation.

Your body is made of what you are fascinated with and where you are living from. There is no death. Growing is deepening and deepening in the fascination. Streams and streams of that realising change the body and the perception of embodiment. You come upon the crazy notion: "My God, not only do I not die, I am not born! All that was being birthed was the idea of a 'someone', all that is dying is the idea 'I am a someone'. What I Am is ever-present life!"

That fascination begins to shine in the heart and the mind. The mind is no longer dull. You are no longer fascinated with any thought, emotion or any imprint that moves along. You look at them and they evaporate, not because they must, just because you are not fascinated by them anymore.

A little bit of fascination of thought or feeling and you must have it because you are destined to know whatever comes from You. If you are fascinated with the idea that you're a body-mind, you must have it because you're fascinated with it. If you're fascinated with difficulty

and fascinated with separateness, you must have it for
you want to know yourself, thoroughly.

But if you are fascinated with what you deeply first *are*,
then instead of your light, your Knowing, going out to
find a solution for anything, it *is in* and the inner light
opens up your mystery. It is tangible.

Your mystery opens when you give up the idea that you
are a body-mind. Then your body-mind has the kind of
vitality that is not causal or affected.

On retreat or not, I call you into that fascination, letting
go of the fascination with the self. Be fascinated with
where that comes from!

Let Go

Let go of taking turmoil personally. You were taught to
have a peaceful life. There is no such thing. You are the
quietness, you are the peace. You don't need to search
for it. That's bogus. Just keep seeing that all is
happening in *What You Are*.

Alchemy at Work

You know what is taking place, you are awakening to
the deep and that is opening the subconscious, releasing
patterning. Know what is taking place. What is taking
place in the deep is not a process, what is taking place
on the surface seems to be a process but no one is in

process, no one is doing process. It is just alchemy at work realising realisers realising.

Profound Relating as a Constant Living Loving Movement

When we get clear about "What really am I? ", when we are getting clear that we don't actually have a beginning and end, then what is there to fear? Then the body has become open, the heart has become open, the mind has become open, the life becomes open. Much more happens when you are open, because when you are really open, so much more possibility streams and in this, so much more of the subconscious is available to be integrated by such a one.

What I am pointing to is: there is no one here but that One who is aware and knowing. In not pushing away the subconscious, deeper doors of possibility open and instead of having contained relationships we *are* profound relating as a constant breathing, living, loving movement that has entrance into profound realisation and profound form, moving, dancing, living, loving.

Deeper embodiment is when the heart is fully opened in this moment to a greater knowing of 'What Is'. When one is relating in this moment, to each other and to this moment of life, then instead of having re-call through memory we are called to Being.

When We Need Comfort

When we need comfort, we create stories to cover our
heart and our pain of not being able to meet the
subconscious in the belief that the subconscious has
something to do with what we are. But really it is just
moved by the greater movement of the unfolding of
one's true nature.

Like a stone can be carved into a great sculpture or
material can be turned into a garment, you are working
this out. This is your life, working out What 'I' actually
Am, awakening to deeper Knowing and meaning. No
longer making stories about it as I move What I Am up
into a self that has conditioning in it, as it should,
because if it was fixed I wouldn't know my eternal
nature, because I just realise more and more of What I
Am. This form here is to take the form of What I Am.
This is why everything is in change, but 'I' am not.

All is Made of What You Are

As you awaken you realise that all this movement has
nothing to do with anything that is personal. Somehow
it is returning you to You, to realise *What You Are*, not
as someone here, but everyone is That realising itself,
on this level in form but deeper in light. It is all made of
light and that is the light of Awareness.
Until a greater knowledge is touched upon or opened to,
on this level there is a tendency to feel shame or guilt,
blame or blaming, but that is still a play of this greater
movement of Self-realisation. One cannot extract
oneself from this play, other than realise that this play is

made of You, and then why would you want to extract yourself from it? You realise you are actually not *of* it. As Awareness you then have entrance to a deeper realm of your own Being that you are realising.

For the light that streamed from You-Awareness is the Self that you are seeking. You want to know every level of yourself. So you are moving in all the levels of yourself, knowing yourself. That is Self-fulfillment, Self-enlightenment. That is realising the Self. You are not 'someone', you are Awareness, which is the Absolute from which light came forth so that Awareness could know it is aware and Knowing could be aware of Knowing. That is the light of Awareness.

All ideas that anyone is guilty fall away from you. At some point you realise no one is to blame, no-one is guilty, you realise that *What You Are* has no opposites. All is made of *What You Are*. That really begins to calm and rest down in the depth and you realise you are the depth.

Then your Seeing and Knowing is not made of a 'someone' with objects and goals and orientation of having or getting or getting rid of. You are 'What Is'. You are not at peace. You *are* peace. You are not in love, you *are* Love, you are not telling the truth, you *are* Truth.

No One Goes Through the Eye of the Needle

Q: *When I hear you and what you are pointing to, I know you are coming from having been through the eye of the needle. I want to get to that point.*

B: No one goes through the eye of a needle. No one. Awareness identified with form and gathering conceptual forms of identity, when it is over the belief that form can give it anything as a separate sense, looks back from whence it came into the light of its Knowing. The light of its Knowing is not distance, it is now. But in the beyond, known forms, thought-forms cannot pass through into the thought-less. So even the 'I-thought' has to dissolve and the thought that 'I have things' has to dissolve.

If you just look at your own life, you will see how much your belief tree has been shaken from holding patterns of separation. You will see how this has enabled you to know yourself more sweetly and dearly and know others more sweetly and dearly, beholding the dilemma of apparent humanness. What one is passing through as the 'eye of the needle' is simply going into the unknown. The unknown is what one is, unknown. You are passing through that.

When one is awakening, what is sparked within, is a deeper Knowing than your usual thought-sense and your usual action, something deeper captures your heart. Instead of just reacting and holding onto the known, something takes place that is so real or surreal and you respond to Knowing although it is unknown. You just know to respond to it. It doesn't have sense-form but you know it is calling and it is the deeper level of You calling, the unknown level of You, the formless level of You. That is through the 'I', just 'I' with no 'Am' on it.

You are passing through that and it is in daily life. Somehow your tree is being shaken or you are simply dismissing or not using thought-forms, emotional forms and old ways. You are letting them go, you are awakening to greater reality, formless.

But all this is made of the formless, for You are the formless just misidentified with form through thought, feeling and belief. It is conditional but You are the unconditional and in being true to your unconditional nature, conditions change, as they do, for you are the key to change all conditions, not because you need to change them, just that when you are true to the other side of your heart, your being, then this side changes. It is not a change of thought, it is a change of allegiance to a deeper place of Being or moving. You are being true to the unspeakable that calls you, but You *are* the unspeakable that is calling you.

Day Thirteen

*"Every star you see in the sky is a perfect match for
every cell and neuron in your mind and body.
It's a star alignment. Your body is a sleeping giant, your
mind is a sleeping genius and your heart is a sleeping
star."*

A Walking Abyss

Q: *I have been watching myself heading towards an
abyss within and what arises in me is terror and I watch
myself trying to identify with something to get out of
that terror.*

B: The abyss is simply the unknown and the self is
simply the known and You are both. It's all made of
You. The known level of self cannot go into the
unknown level of You. It's not your self heading
towards the abyss, it's You. You do the same every
single night. You move from something to no thing.
You are doing it now but during the day, can you not
see it? It is all that's happening.

There is one teaching: 'The Course in Miracles' where
they call this the 'holy instant'. It's a holy instant, which
means in this moment now, this instant is whole, it is
not in parts. It is wholly what Awareness is, whether it
is in the experience of form or in the experience of
nothing, the experience is Awareness knowing it knows;
wherever it is, for all eternity.

It is You in the level of self moving to manifest your self from your unknown quality of Being. Right there is where you stop and you have fear. You are only fearing You. Keep seeing during the day that you are moving from the known into the deeper levels of You, to your self unknown but to You: Knowing.

During the day you move from a self that is known, because that's the way you have made it until you are in it cleanly, which means: each day you wake up new, each moment you wake up new. In each conversation you are new and not yesterday's conversation. You are what you're realising in the abyss, the deeper You. You are realising it 'now' and it is coming up and having form. Every day you *are* the abyss walking and there are moments when you don't realise you are in the deep, in the abyss; there is no self.

You might just be enjoying what appears to your mind to be Truth but you are in the bliss of this level of You. You just don't realise that you *are*, right then, the abyss being the serenity. You might still observe the trees, but the observation or the Knowing of the tree is made of the bliss You Are, made of the abyss You Are.

For you in that moment, sitting on that hill, there is no separation between the unknown and 'now'. No separation until your self gets involved, that you think about your self, that your self names the hill, names the tree, names the experience as good, bad, hot or cold. You are a walking abyss, a freedom. That is what You Are. There are moments when you identify some fragment and that's where your fear is.

The Very First Room

Here we are all assembled but did you know this is not assembly room? This is a disassembling room. Here there is nothing but disassembling going on. Not disabling but *enabling* is happening through disassembling. Enabling through disassembling. Welcome to the disassembling room. Which room of yours do you notice that disassembles you and which rooms of yours are not disassembling rooms but enabling rooms? Have a look.

It looks like we're all gathered in this room but this room has no walls, has no ceilings has no floors. Pure Awareness, no room. Rooms kind of happen when light comes from nowhere and it is only in the room that Awareness knows it is knowing it is aware.

From Knowing many other rooms come into being and then into manifestation, but Awareness is able to move into all the rooms, knowingly aware and it doesn't need any of them.

I am very clear, we're all the same One, very clear that that we are the very first room. That's how we are able to know, that first room being The Self, Pure Knowing, but then there are many rooms, unchangeable rooms and changing rooms but they're all known by Awareness who is without beginning or end and is the Absolute, is the one that is listening to these words now.

In ordinary everyday life Awareness can know whether it's in a changing room or whether it's coming from a room where there is no change within this changing room. Somehow this room of changing re-forms from the non-changing room or deeper reality. It just happens and suddenly all the rooms are filled with that that never happens and that is the one listening to these words now.

Up in this changing room it is ridiculous trying to stop the changes. They *are* going to happen, constantly. What is even more ridiculous is identifying with this changing room but if you look, there is one who is knowing all the rooms and that one doesn't change.

In existence the changing room is perceived and known by Knowing itself that does not change. It's fruitless and pointless to hang onto that that keeps changing, this changing room of humanness. But nonetheless this room is made out of that that doesn't change and that that doesn't change is the maker of this room, the designer of this room and the dissolver of this room. You can come all the way in and realise You Are the changeless, the light of Awareness.

Satsang

Satsang is communion *as* Truth, not two. Often what we do is we relate to the horizontal. Truth is vertical, then it appears on the horizontal. If you have a look on the horizontal you will see where you have sown seeds of Truth or greater seeds of Reality. You have sown them, You who is aware. But many other seeds are sown in there too, seeds of wanting, seeds of needing, seeds of expectation. You could call them 'world seeds', they're distracting. But it is the seeds of Reality that are calling you. What happens in satsang is that all those seeds, regardless of whether they are distracting or not, false or real, are all brought 'here', because 'here' Nothing matters to Truth.

Then in your life you see that something is changed within the appearance of the horizontal, just by being deeply true. You don't need it to be different. It just changes to match what you're coming into, which is Nothing. All answers are found in your heart only.

True Enquiry

Q: *Can you speak about true enquiry? I always thought that enquiry on some level uses thought.*

We're moving as aware Seeing and Knowing, we're not using any faculty of the body-mind self or person. We are direct Awareness seeing and knowing. The kind of seeing and knowing that still remains when you're in deep dreamless sleep and that will remain when the body drops away. When everything is taken away: pure Seeing, pure Knowing, sweetness is present and it is *You*.

True enquiry is dropping away enquiring with a movement of mind, with a movement of a sense of self through emotion, with all the movements of anything that belongs to the body-mind. You're enquiring directly with *What You Are*. You suspend looking backwards in time or looking forward in hope. You look within and as you settle down in a more quieted space within, what arises is a deeper Knowing and a deeper Seeing that is

really the sweetness of our being. It might not yet
appear sweet, but it is the sweetness of our being. We're
meeting our being and remembering that our being is
the radiance of our Self.

Enquiry is first off with your heart and then deeper. You
are listening to what the heart picks up from the unseen.
You're not interested in sense-perception but now you
will be able to perceive deeper than sense-perception.
Your inner perception will turn around and turn into
sense-perception like it does when you wake up in the
morning.

You *can* enquire with multi-dimensional Awareness
splitting. In that manner your enquiry is bypassing your
sense of self and reaching into the deep of you. You
have been prepared for this moment! It doesn't just take
you to passionately want to know deeper, you have to
have a sense of true enquiry, true investigation. For you
to even look within in that manner, means your life has
been emptying you out in some way or other through
circumstances. It has been detaching you from believing
you are a 'someone'. So when you look in, that is your
light, and rather than going into thought and feeling it is
going out into present Awareness-Knowing. You begin
to pick up a deeper Knowing and it resonates in your
Awareness.

As you deepen into that enquiry you can actually
enter it. You are able to be fully entered in this and turn
around and enter the 'more than this' and whilst you
have a form on this level, this *'entering'* you come into,
is able to flow up to this level and they become one.
More and more you don't use the human intellect,

thought or feeling or any newscast to move by. It now
all belongs to this deeper Knowing and the enquiry
continues until you become more and more stabilised in
the inner, rather than moving from what you believe is
outside.

So enquiry is with your heart first, through your
Awareness in your heart. Your heart begins to receive
the deeper levels and then you flow the deeper levels
through the radiance of your heart. Here you *bring* it up
into the formed level and your form is made different.
Until this body can be completely opened in any one
moment and your being has entrance to pour into this
level, filling you up. Now you are knowing the
sweetness of Pure Being.

Day Fourteen

*"Space or emptiness defines its forms,
its forms do not define the emptiness."
Mind thinks objects define 'What Is'
but it is space that defines 'What Is'
and manifests 'What Is'."*

No Relationship

It is quite something to have no relationship whatsoever
with your mind. It is quite something to have no
relationship with emotion. It is even more extraordinary
to have no relationship with what appears to be in this
space called Awareness. No thoughtful relationship that
is, or no emotional relationship. The mind sees it as
cold, not to have a relationship with thought or feeling
but actually it is very warm.

We value thought and feeling because that puts our
relatedness into a relationship to ourselves. But in truth
there is no relationship that will ever work.
Relationships are solid blocks. Relating is only in the
moment. Relation-ship is dependent on past, future
thought and feeling, determined by a relationship to
someone that doesn't actually exist.

Your First Relationship

Here we are sitting in this room. Please be very clear as
to your *first* relationship. Your first relationship is to the
belief you are somebody, sitting next to another

somebody. See how powerful that is. It is extremely powerful, so powerful that it makes it real. But it's not real. It is a level of reality but it is *Reality* coming together at a point of circumference, a point of Knowing that can speak to an apparent other point of Knowing and these two points point to one place where the Real relating begins and the Real relating ends and continues to begin and end. It is that beginning and ending that is the pulse in your wrist or the pulse in a star or the impulse to ever be together.

So once again, just to affirm this in your own consciousness, your own awareness, your first relationship, until you have seen deeper or transcended, is to your use of thought and feeling to define *What You Are*.

Thought and feeling is not the *first* that defines *What You Are*, it is the *last* of what defines you on this plane.

What *first* defines *What You Are* is that you are aware and you are knowingly aware. That is your first definition.

Now, if you really see this, that your first definition of *What You Are* is that you are aware and you are *knowingly* aware, something really begins to take place. You need to be *knowingly* aware to know 'What Is'. Knowing-Awareness or Awareness- Knowing is the very spaciousness in which all objective appearance, including this level of body-mind, appears.

Defining What You Are

What is the relationship between your body and any other body, whether it be a wall, a floor, an insect or a mountain? What is the relationship between what you appear to be there right now and any other object? What is your relationship? If your first relationship is the object of that body or another, a thought or another thought, a feeling or another feeling, you have defined yourself in limitation. You have defined *What You Are* in limitation. So you are already moving as a limited sense of Knowing-Awareness, limited to a form in a space that is already defining the universe, for the universe *is* defined in a space.

You couldn't know a star, you couldn't know a planet, you couldn't know a body, couldn't know another, couldn't know a flower, a wall, a floor, a ceiling. Space or emptiness defines its forms. Its forms do not define the emptiness. The objects in this room do not define the space. We can remove all the objects and the space is always that that remains; Pure Awareness.

We are used to defining what we are through objects, objectives. We put the objects in the room, the colour, the picture on the wall, the person in it, you, the furniture, our art, our technique, our medicine, our this, our that. But it is the space that defines 'What Is' and the objects appear in it, for they are made of the space and it is the space that manifests the objects. All objects come from space and return to space, come from the void and return to the void, come from the vacuum and return to the vacuum.

Creative Source and Power

Within this vacuum, or this Nobody-ness, is ultimate power, ultimate Knowing purely aware. This means that the one who is listening to these words now is its own creative source and power, creating and dissolving whilst redefining What It Is because there is no beginning or end to the one who is listening to these words now.

That Space is 'You'

Between what you appear to be and let's say, the wall, is space. That space is *You*, using space as a definition of infinite Awareness. That space is You. And the appearance of You is You *as* that space, defining what you are on this level, manifest. Only on this level, not on other levels. On deeper levels of Reality or space, you are able to define yourself more purely but on this level you are discovering how *What You Are* on *this* level moves; a spiralling of energy and forms come into existence. As aware Knowing you are redefining *What You Are* on this level in form.

Your relationship is not with your body-mind, your relationship is with that in which your body stands: space. And within the space of your body and the space of a wall, the space of another and the space between a thought or a feeling is *You*.

Within that space, within that movement I described as a spin, is profound energy making it possible to manifest how Awareness-Knowing is defining What It

Is on this level of manifestation. That is producing a tremendous amount of energy, the same amount of energy as the entire manifestation of the cosmos is in a single cell in your body. Ultimate energy within every cell of the body, holding the definition on this level of What I Am.

Real Experience

Being present, aware in Knowing, in other words, 'I am Awareness-Knowing it knows it is aware', is real experience.

Relating to that is not a relationship, it is Now. Relating to that ultimate power is within our hands. *As* Nothing, ultimate power is moving, manifesting, undoing and remaking. This is what is happening in the cells of your body and this is what is happening in the cells of the universe and the cells of the entire cosmos.

The Self is redefining itself because it has no beginning or end and its relating is to ultimate Awareness or the Absolute.

In dancing The Form, looking into blackness or even walking down the street in the emptiness, you are pulling ultimate energy as a Beingness to manifest your relationship with Knowing-Aware and it is manifesting in your daily life.

The Universe is Your Body

The universe is also your body. It arises the same time as this physical body. This body arises, the universe arises. You go to sleep, the universe for you is not there. That's really how it is.

You are moving. You are a living movement of Awareness, seamless. There is no sleep. In truth you don't sleep, it is just that you have trained your Awareness only in sense-things, painful things distractive things and so, when you go to sleep you don't stay aware, knowingly aware.

At some point you will begin to see that there is no sleep. You move into deeper dimensions, or all the way home as aware Knowing. Then you come back here. It's actually not that you come *back* here. All this is part of your shining body, that you are exploring. Just like you are exploring this life, you are exploring your totality too, You who is Awareness in the body of Knowing.

Your real body is a body of Pure Being, it is a 'christed' body or a buddha body; a body of *living* Awareness.

Tuscany Retreat

"It is the unfamiliar that is your Love, not the familiar.
The unfamiliar brings you alive and awake.
Where you are uncontained is
where you are truly safe.
The familiar is not safe, it dies, it passes away.
The unfamiliar does not pass away.
Those that live in an unfamiliar
subtle way of Being will not pass away."

Opening Night

"None of us are truly realising the tremendous power of the moment. The power of this moment is the same power that manifests moves and lives and returns the universe."

The Edge of Identity

When uncertainty turns up, the program in the psyche is to reach into the past and make the moment certain from past perspectives. Awareness (you and I), that is building and evolving humanness, is integrating past into the profound opportunity for what is truly present and then one builds the need to continue in comfort.

Uncertainty brings opportunity because that uncertainty is not going to build the moment from the past. Uncertainty takes you on the edge of your identity. You can move beyond your believed identity, that means uncertainty moves your awareness into the deep, the unknown, the uncreated, what you truly really are. Uncertainty gives you all that you are in the deep. Right there on the edge of identity, past is undone and the deep is made into form.

A moment of uncertainty can become a precious singular moment for you. It is where you choose to be fully awake and conscious on the cutting edge of your identity, no longer definitely 'someone' from a believed certainty that the past has supplied you, thoughts, feelings, experiences charged with 'positive and negative' within your body-mind.

The moment you move as Awareness all those levels move as you and each level speaks through you, sees and hears through you and better: sees *for* you, hears for you speaks for you walks and talks for you. You are not being You, you are being your past. Uncertainty ends this and puts the power back into You as Being.

The Deep Begins to Live

The very power that moves and manifests the universe, the stars the planets, the living of all these beings is moved and manifests in a singular moment called Now.

That is the same power Awareness uses to identify its familiar sense of self. You are holding it all together. It is in moments when Awareness is clearly uncertain that this moment becomes free of any past recurrence.

The power that moves and manifests the universe then moves and manifests the depth, which Awareness is now entering. The deep begins to live.

Imprints of Belief

The body-mind is an amazing instrument; it has many layers and levels. We take for granted what a body is. Really, we don't know ourselves deep enough to realise the super-sensitivity of each level of our body and that it absorbs what Awareness is believing in. It imprints it in each level of the body, mind, emotion, nervous system, in the cells of the body and even the brain.

All those imprints, all those programs move the moment Awareness moves. You are moving now, just by listening you are a movement of Awareness and the moment Awareness moves light happens; the body-mind is manifesting. In each moment you are imprinting into levels of the body-mind your belief system.

Day One

*"In real recognition there is openness and within
openness the field resolves quite naturally.
What we may call weeds, old crops or old thought-
patterns, when simply noticed, dissolve.
All resolves in openness."*

Tending to the Field

Humans have no idea that they create 'a field', because
our tendency is to really believe that we are human. But
we are Being first, then human. *Being*-human.
You may or may not have looked at life like this. Have
you noticed the field around a newly born baby? Even
the parents become new! They have this tender
tendency to have a great deal of care. The whole house
begins to be full of care and that house begins to vibrate
in a new field. This vibratory field is no different to the
field you can see out there with grass growing in it.

What you plant in a manifest field will grow. You might
have a crop in a field and unless you really cleared that
field, last year's crop will come through. A very old
crop from ten years will still be struggling to come
through and the ground, which you call a field, may not
even be good enough to grow anything.

Our tendency is to keep our Awareness and our light of
Knowing in an old field of experience. So we point our
Awareness into the familiar and that old field is very

mixed. It has many different old crops in it and all manner of weeds.

Maybe the ground is struggling to keep the whole field growing.

But notice when you see a newborn, that everyone around this child will spend their time cleaning up the field, on many different levels, not just dirty diapers! It is their old manner, their old behaviours they pick up. There is a level of cleansing and renewal taking place.

You can go so much deeper than that and I know that this is why we are together here. We are together to discover the potential of this field and to discover that we are in a much, much profoundly bigger field and that field has been prepared.

I am pointing you to the greater possibility that we have in this field. It is not so much pulling out the old crop, pulling out the old weeds and the labour of that. It is much more simple. It is recognition. Simply recognising.

In real recognition there is openness and within openness the field is resolved quite naturally. What we may call weeds or old crops, when simply noticed, dissolve. All resolves in openness.

When Awareness has a preference of a crop that was planted many years ago, then the experience is mixed. There is clearly the longing for the new but Awareness isn't discerning the new from the old.

Are you ready? Because you haven't seen my plough as yet and there is nothing like my combined harvester! It is combined with Love and tenderness, goodness, clarity and meaning. To the mind it will seem to have sharp hooks and blades but to the heart it is like being caressed by a warm breeze.

Now the field has changed. Can you see it? Instead of sitting in our old rooted positions, like an old carrot over here, an old potato over there and a piece of celery over there, something has changed. When the field changes, the experience shines the new.

Going Deeper

When Awareness begins to awaken, then what is awakening is the unknown, the deep. Awareness is awakening to deeper Knowing than experience. This is what I refer to as 'The Calling'. I also say that *this* is the possibility: Love knowing, moving manifesting the deep.

Even as we speak now, as Awareness, for we are Awareness, we know this is a room by the light of our Knowing. Knowing on the surface objectifies Knowing. We know we are in a very large white room with a certain amount of people. That is an objectified Knowing. If we are going just a little bit deeper, but it is shallow, we can know from the subconscious, still objectified for it divides everything and everyone into a 'like and dislike'.

If we go just a little bit deeper than that and if we are prepared to dive deep into the unknown, there is pure Knowing and it has no objects on a manifest level. It is Pure Knowing, Pure Being.

Awareness can get wonderfully lost in the depth of its own Knowing. When Awareness is lost in the deep, it finds What It Is, not an object but the power in which all this shines, moves and has meaning.

Going deeper, Knowing is not objectified and Awareness knows it knows more than surface experience. Awareness, you have just transcended your separate sense of self and the field now is prepared on the surface. In its preparation the subconscious comes up to the surface.

When we really begin to awaken, objectified experience begins to crumble and the consciousness that has been functioning and operating only on the surface, will think it is dying. So the consciousness on the surface begins to trade places with the sub-conscious that is moving everything secretly.

There is a kind of an agreement that happens. Your surface consciousness comes down into your subconsciousness. You-Awareness become conscious of your subconscious and your subconscious comes up to the surface, where it feels incredibly vulnerable and naked with nowhere to hide.

This is the seed and beginning of the pure tree of life. Suddenly, when those two are trading place, Awareness, which is the one listening to these words now, and

Knowing, the light of Awareness, is awakening to its profound mystery. You will be experiencing this exchange. *That* is self-transformation.

Whilst Awareness will not remain awake in this switch-over, you will be feeling a lot of pain and difficulty, but when Awareness stays open to all of what is really here, its light begins to shine. Now there is no need to keep the surface and the sub-conscious apart. Your secret pains are now known. Your distractions are known. Your hopes, desires, dreams, nightmares and failures, they are all out in the open. There is a completely new power in this. It is the power of Love and the field is now ripe for what is more deeply seen and known. Suddenly positive and negative, good and bad, 'he said, she said' has no meaning anymore. In this openness is living possibility and one is alive with no judgment anywhere, whatsoever. An entirely new life is moving.

I Hand You That that is Beyond

There is not a single movement that this body can make that is not a movement of the deep. Discover in your own experience. My hand will move and it's not a hand. It's a movement where I can hand you that that is beyond the hand. My hand will move and I will hold your hand and I will bring you into where hands and bodies and minds and people all disappear. Watch your own movement. It is very much the same but mostly the field of your experience is objectified and it has a wonderful sign above it that says:" What about me?!"

You Cannot Mix What is Deeper With What is Familiar

The deeply true costs us our sub-conscious comfort zones. Be truly deeply seeded in deeper Seeing and Knowing. In allowing the subconscious to be seen and to come home, we truly allow awakening. We cannot mix what is deeper with what is familiar. That is a distortion, but more than that it is human suffering.

We have to un-mix and keep the field growing in what, we are awakening to as Awareness. This starts to change our experience of the body, the self, the person, the mind, the heart. It all begins to change because now it is being transfigured, transformed and a deeper awakening in the unseen is moving up. Not in the distance but in the immediate now. A whole new way is growing. It is not growing in time. It is growing in 'me', this One I Am. Now there is only constant revelation.

Flowering Humans

What I speak of and share isn't just Self-realisation. To me this is only half the deal, realising the beyond and that's it. I am pointing to the integration of what is realised and then a living movement of what is realised, all the way up and out onto the surface and how this can move between two, three, many. If there is enough Freedom in one consciousness, this movement will be within a whole field of flowering humans.

Sexuality Moved by Your Being

Sexuality isn't actually a 'root chakra thing'. It is a 'heart chakra thing'. Energy or sexuality moves cleanly by Being. Whilst one thinks one is a self, energy or sexuality will move for your self. Most people are making a problem of this, because they don't understand what is taking place. When you move by Knowing, that is the light of your being and then sexuality or pure energy forms the movement of Pure Being. In the body that moves and manifests in one movement but in many different spheres.

When sexuality, moved by your being, enters the mind by way of the heart, then your mind will open up to the entire cosmos and your mind will be filled with true light and form. You know, when you see the many little spirals on Buddha's head in statues? I wonder if Buddha ever mentioned that that is the Feminine Principle spiralling out of his Heart-Mind.

An Unfamiliar Subtle Way of Being

See, that we are sitting in an unfamiliar field. Your old way is going to get a little dizzy here. It will be stretching your familiar old way of understanding and interpreting, because this is a subtle transmission. It is not familiar.

It is the unfamiliar that is your Love, not the familiar, The unfamiliar brings you alive and awake. That is where you are really safe, where you are uncontained. The familiar is not safe. It dies, it passes away. The

Unfamiliar does not pass away. Two that make their Love not from the familiar but the unfamiliar, those two will not pass away. All those that live in an unfamiliar subtle way of Being will not pass away.

Singular Freedom

In a deeper dimension you know each other without any boundaries, because there is no need for boundaries. You are perfectly real and good with All that You Are. Nothing needs to be hidden. You are singular Freedom. You are the movement of Love and Light itself. You move uniquely. There is nothing in the deep that separates you from other beings. You are completely unique and in that uniqueness you can *pass through* others.

Here, on this surface level in this moment of evolution, if you don't live 'the normal' you are strange. If you are just a little bit different, you are an outcast but this dimension belongs to the radiance of your original nature and to live fully what you *know* is for you to be fully *What You Are*.

Until the field is enlightened, this level judges everything. On the deeper levels nothing is judged because you are here to live a unique life, you are not supposed to 'toe the line', to live the familiar. You are invited to live the unfamiliar as you become aware of your real Self.

On this level the awakening to your real Self, Awareness, is an evolutionary movement. Some beings are slightly more evolved than apparent others but that doesn't make anyone any different or more or less. All beings are infinite. How your infinity expresses in this finite moment is evolutionary. You are a unique expression of the One.

Fearlessly Alive

Wherever I go, I push the edge. Do you? If you do, you become fearlessly alive. You then will not die. Whilst you are holding on to belief-systems and needing familiar comfort zones, you will die. You will go through the death process. Living the awakening you will not go through the death process. You are making two One.

Stay on the Edge

It is at that edge of your self-identity, as Awareness knowing deeply, that you are able to transform yourself. Only on the edge. You have to stay on it, stay on the edge...

Total Response to Knowing

As you give Knowing total response, your sub-conscious habit of being a particular comfort zone is given up. Then the power that each and every one of us has, which is actually the power of Love or cosmic power, streams new life force into the body-mind. You will no longer be living from imagination, want or need you will be living a divine life; the total response to what you deeply know. Then all this is a manifest form of your original Light.

Beyond the Death Process

Q: When the subconscious rises to surface levels it can really feel like a death process... Can you speak a bit more of this?

B: That is because it *is* the death process. Death is simply the passing away of Awareness identifying with an object. I can guarantee you, when you are dead you still are aware but now your Awareness is free of objective form. You discover that you can move at an incredible speed, free of objective experience. You are moving without the need to move from past. You realise you are free of moving as a sense of self. You go: "Oh my God, I was moving as through I was some body, now I can move as Being!"

So you *are* going through a death process but all that can die is the false, not You. You are the Real. Even your separate sensed experiences of: "I am hurting. You are terrible. What are you doing to me?" All this is only real because You are the light of Reality. Everything is real, positive or negative, because *You* are the Real. Anything that you give attention to and then identification, becomes real even though it is false, because *You* are the light of Reality. *You* are the Reality behind all experience.

Eventually you tire of making the false real, but you will have another good go at making it real. You can make it real for quite a while, but all objective experience is a projection only. You are the Real free of projection. When you cease projecting You are the profound Reality that truly is. "

You are dying to the objects of experience, such as your body, your mind, your sense of self and person. They are objects within your own awareness that build around you. To become like a child you need to have pure innocent form which doesn't move as past experience but as present Awareness.

As Awareness, everything that you have in your Awareness, such as a body, a sense of self and person and even the world, registers in You. You are like a beacon of light passing through all those forms. And any movement within any level of your body-mind registers. In any moment you can have a thought register, a feeling register and you can see in the registration of thought or feeling: "What quality is it? Is it a clear thought or does it contain past?"

You realise in the registration of that feeling whether it is a pure feeling or a feeling of attachment. As Awareness, you are registering the evolution of every level of the body-mind and its development and whether the evolution matches what You first Are. Otherwise you are going to have to identify with each of those levels as if they were 'you'. You will be lost in self-concern.

"Amazing Grace, I once was blind and now I see." See this, it is happening! You are unblinding yourself. You will see and know yourself like you never did before. If you don't judge yourself you experience the death of the old pattern. Right there your pure being will fill that level up with Love.

Everything is being registered but *You* are free of registration. This is knowing yourself. If there is pain, guilt shame or whatever it is, all that you are really registering is a wave of Pure You, having experience. It doesn't matter that that wave seems to move in positive and negative. It matters that that *is* a wave of *You*. It lived! It is your mind that projects it as positive and negative. When you fully let a positive or negative live, only then will you be free of polarity.

If you make death a process, you need to move by processing. You can just come directly to the heart. Then the relating to 'process' will look entirely different. Processing is the shifting and reshaping of the forms of the light of Knowing. That is what is at play in the universe. Seeing and Knowing is not related to time and space. It is related to the deep, the place-less place you as Awareness resolve into in deep dreamless sleep. It is profoundly real.

Relate first to the deeper Seeing and Knowing. Come up through the heart and relate the deeper Seeing and Knowing to the actuality of the surface. That is the growing of a new seed cracking the surface.

Fully Awake Whilst Your Old House Falls Into Ruins

What it looks like to stay awake in a death process? Let me describe it like this, whilst your old house falls into ruins, you are able to continue as if nothing ever happened in the light of the movement of the awakening. You don't need to dodge the roof as it collapses through your head. You don't need to let it miss you. As your old house collapses it passes through you, it doesn't touch you. If it touches you, you must feel the touch totally but then not move from how it touched you. Until the whole universe can collapse and you still walk amongst its ruins.

The truth is we love the ruination. We can actually be fully awake in the collapse of the old house. It brings a fire of Love and an ability to move as if we only exist right here and now, because we do! A hand that used to ache with the pain of the past is then able to pass on living knowledge, living Love. Suddenly we have these abilities of our deeper awakened-ness.

This is tested without there being a test, in the old house collapsing in ruins. Don't bother picking up the old bricks. No, put the new house together from an entirely different place. It really doesn't matter that others see you as if you existed in the past. You exist Now and you can dance how you dance Now. That is the true meaning of having life, like a river flowing from an endless ocean, unidentified with past or space or time.

If the house that collapses touches you, then there are still more doors to collapse. Perhaps the floor hasn't caved in as yet. The floor is your sexuality, which is pure energy. If your energy still belongs to an old movement you are still standing on your past. Ultimately discover that *You* are manifesting *all* your experience. Ultimately! It is all in manifestation because of what You truly Are. If anything can touch you, you are still objectifying experience and not bringing it back to Knowing. You are free as Love by not objectifying experience. Then all objects are made of that Love.

No Need to Understand

The wonderful thing with this life, when you become sensitive enough, is that there is no need to understand anything or anybody. There is just Being, sensitive and open to the truth that the body is a transmission of Source.

Resistance is Attention to Self-image

Give attention to a self-image and you have resistance. Because the image is made out of resistance. The movement of life and its forms is not, it is a river of light. Within the flow of that river there is no image and no resistance. An image is a snapshot of the experience of Now. And once you make a snapshot of Now, you are able to look back through the snapshot as if all those images are you. But *You* have already moved on.

What is that image, and what is that resistance? Quite simple: comparison! You are comparing 'what was' to 'What Is'. That is resistance and the building of a mask, an image. You are teaching your mind to compare every moment with past experience. But your mind wasn't built for images, it is built to stay wide open and, through it and your heart, manifest the light of your being. These images are all that you are called to dissolve by being true Now.

The moment You Awareness move, whilst you have form, the entire energy that manifests the universe moves with you. And you infuse the image with energy making it real. You make the self-image believable. Just add a few images to that and you are streaming images but your light is passing through them all.

Your power of creativity, which is your pure sexuality, is maintaining a self-image. You are re-creating it. That is the resistance you feel when you begin to awaken. Giving this power back to your heart dissolves the self-image. It dissolves through You as Awareness being true to pure Knowing. Knowing is the light of your Self. All images are dissolved in being true to Knowing. Try it and see.

More Than a Miracle

What You Are is an oceanic river of life, not a person. You are more than a miracle. Your self-image is using up the energy and building more images of a separate sense of self. Remove the image and clearly, the ocean will move the river, and the river will move the life. And when the ocean moves the river and the river moves the life, there is a figure eight: infinite flow of Being and Forming. Then the Self is the constant

realisation and life is its constant loving movement. It is
one tremendous flow of openness and tenderness.
Remove the image, you will feel a resurgence of new
life. Let the images dissolve.

Sleeping Beauty Awakening

How about if there *is* just beauty, wonder, mystery in
everyone you could possibly ever meet? You could be a
sleeping beauty, waiting for a kiss; a kiss of being true
from *You*. That would be awakening.

New Life is Now

What is it that is just beyond these images? Well, these
images must be living through light. What if that light
could move through those images and not belong to
them?

Notice how in this moment you, like I, have registered a
deeper connection. You may have registered a deeper
connection in the unseen and a deep connection within
the body. The ground is prepared for the new life, which
is not distant - it is Now. All your images, you can just
let them go. It is going to live as if you never existed
before this moment. This is the truth, it has got an
entirely different life, You, who is Awareness, you will
not need a physical death to live an entirely new life.

Good God...

Image and comparison create fear and that gets locked
in space and time. The moment that gets locked in space
and time and locked into your body-mind, you distance
you from You being the Source of All That Is. Then
God is something in the distance and so is the Good.
But good God, you *are* that Good.

You Are the Immensity

This idea that you are somebody who can't handle
anything is an illusion, a self-image. How did you get
here in the body? This will have your mind working
something out on a biological level but biology is a
metaphysical movement and the metaphysical is a
movement of light and the movement of light is a
movement of Truth. The metaphysical is the movement
of the beyond.

That moves and in an instant *all this* appears. Truly, the
biological body is a metaphysical movement. The
transcendental is moving all this, biologically,
metaphysically and manifest. We could meet there right
now and if we keep going deeper we will be the same
One, realising what It is. All is made of the light of
Awareness moving.

The moment you believe you are someone doing this,
then you are just in the surface, identified with the
biology. Your surface pain will be mental and
emotional to do with something in space and time.

If you are a little deeper, the surface pain is a movement of the profound. The mind turns it into pain but it is the movement and change within the metaphysical, biological coming up to the surface. We are profound manifestors, mistakenly identified with the idea of being 'someone'.

From the smallest Knowing the cosmos manifests. Getting mixed up with the belief you are 'someone' makes you feel helpless amongst so much immensity. But you are the immensity and not helpless. Simply put, you don't need to fix anything but you do need to let it fall apart. When it all falls apart You remain and then it all reforms in the light of your own awareness.

Peel Back the Covers!

We can be lazy and keep all our nice images tucked up in bed or we can wake up whilst still in bed, peel back the covers and *be* living, moving Awareness. That means everything that you are giving so much value to is false. It all passes away. It is *You* that doesn't pass away. You are Reality, not all the images you have coated yourself in.

I Am Here Now

It seems impossible for you to move without image. But you do already, most definitely in deeper realms. Be here now. Now is infinite. Infinite means there is no limitation to what is here now. I Am here now.

In allowing that in, you fall endlessly into the deep. No need to hang on to the last word or the last image. It is what you love. You don't love hanging on. You're fed up with hanging on. You love letting loose. Falling in.

Beyond the Prism of the Mind

Either Awareness is looking through the prism of the mind, which will create an image on the glass, the lens of experience, or you are not looking through the prism of the mind. You are knowing Knowing direct, you have not shrunk Reality, You *are* It.

This will shatter the glass of your self-image. Then you have no need of any more glass, no need of any image. You won't shrink anymore in the openness of what truly is. You are no longer deluding *What You Are*. You will stand free. Standing free is now.

Looking through the mind you think your experience was of the past, but all experience is in the now. And the now doesn't need any glass to paint, it doesn't view through a lens. Without the lens of an image Awareness, you are knowing, seeing, realising the deep!

Nothing that is real can break. Look through the mind and you will create a past and then you will create a story of the past. You are painting on the lens of perception and you are painting someone who is perceiving, someone who is experiencing in space and time.

But the experience is 'I Am now'. As now, you grow in greater depths of perception, and your Seeing and Knowing belongs to the deep. Having a body is the manifestation of that Love. It is deep Love. Simply stop looking through the lens of the crystallisation of your mind.

I am endeavouring to point you towards not building the need of a future to get this. Be so open, that you are sinking into the greater depth of knowing yourself. Then there is nothing that can ever take place or move that is not Love moving.

Moving Without a Centre

Can you see, know and move without a centre? *That* is openness. First, you come back to a centre called 'I'. Before that, you have a centre called 'I Am', and before that you have a centre called 'I am someone'. In Awakeness you step back to 'I'. Then the perception is through a centre called 'I' but that centre still has a deeper invitation within it and that is to lose your centre.

You move to this in deep dreamless sleep. This is when you are fully open and not self-centered. If you look at this deeply, even your 'I' will disappear. Then you are like when you were a child, no sense of 'I', yet so sweet and tender and open. That is your original nature. You can be so open that what pours out is the light of Awareness and the light of Awareness can receive all the images and forms on their return. That is the movement of infinite Knowing-Aware.

Remain Open

I am not going to tell you to let go. It is impossible to let go. There is no one there to let go. *What You Are* can remain open amongst everything that moves. You stay open. Your old way is returning into the openness. Instead of just continuing an image going around in a circle, the consciousness, which is life, the energy that you made an image of, returns. You are the door to the deep and the door to the forming. You will experience this within your body.

No Reference

Can you move without any reference? Is that your deepest desire? Yes? When you make this your movement in life, you have undone the usual you. Now you are entering Pure You. As you enter Pure You, that is the transformation of your self. Now you are growing your ability to be the living tree of newness, where your branches go up into the sky and your roots down into the earth.

When you get really clear that this is the direction you want to go in, you will go slowly in it, you will be acutely aware of the breath and the reading of the deeper spheres and the reading of the direct Knowing. You will come alive in it.

You will enjoy being a child once again. It will be as if you are learning to walk without any support. You will be walking the new. When you were a child you didn't use your self to walk. You didn't use the person to walk.

Your enjoyment was just 'walking'. Now you are moving this fresh, new, innocent aliveness. When you live that now, you are living the new life.

Truly Die to Truly Live
The Form Reality Practice

Those that are ready to truly live, are those that are ready to truly die. Those that are ready to truly die, truly live. Make your choice clear. See the enjoyment of that knowledge. That is you being lived as Being.

As we move in just a taste of The Form this is exactly what we are looking at. The Form is not something that you practice in the past. The Form is what you live now. It is not something you practiced last week or last year. It is you being so awake in your innermost, all the way out to the form of your self, that when you move, you are not moving through a sense of self, you are moving direct as a being. Then your movement is not a concern of how you move as a body, as a self, your movement is how you move as Being. No self-referencing.

When you practice The Form with no self-referencing you are free of all the objects, even though there is a person sitting on the chair. You are not objectifying the other. The other is in the dance of Being. That is the transmission, and that is the deeper unfolding.

Embodiment is Now
The Form Reality Practice

If you truly observe during the day, when you go to
sleep or in the morning, in your Awareness you will
watch the body being built *now*. You will also see that
the whole of nature is manifesting in you in the now.
You will watch forms just coming from nothing to light,
to form. While you are still so preoccupied with your
sense of self you miss the pure perception that
embodiment is now.

Movement is Formless
The Form Reality Practice

Within the movements of The Form, you discover that
movement is formless and *then* converted into form.
That conversion of the Formless makes known to you
an embodiment of what is deeper than form.
This unlocks the idea that you are someone in
particular. It opens to the spaciousness that you
are; Pure Being. Everything. You begin to see that this
body is a timeless movement of your awareness. The
body then is no longer limited. It was limited by the
belief that you are a body. When you are realising you
are not the body, the body is no longer a fixed formed
identity, it is able to move. You are registering levels of
deeper Awareness, unseen levels of your inner
dimensions.

Open to All That Is
The Form Reality Practice

When I am open to all that is and to all people I am
communicating with, then I can drop deeper, deeper
than the sense of self. Then I communicate from the
deeper body of Love or Awareness. Whilst I have form,
that body comes with a speed beyond mind
comprehension up to the surface.

What you are seeing when I move is way, way deeper
than your mind. That is why one man said that "I Am
the way". You discover *You* Are the way. You are way,
way deeper than your mind, and you are able to move in
the beyond and up to the surface in the same manner.
And you can immediately speak of it, because it is in
your experience.

When we come to The Form, your perception changes.
Instead of functioning as somebody with a past, you
have the opportunity to drop deep down within. Maybe
then you realise, that your hands that move are a
movement prior to the belief there are hands moving
and that your feet that move, are actually the
manifestation of walking in a deeper dimension.

What is Age?

What the body is, is the forming of the deep. The mind
tells you that the body has age but the mind is a liar.
The body has no age. Age is the distance you put
between what you know you are and what you believe
you are. That is age. It is the distance you put between

the truth you know You are and your self-experience
that you are continually believing. Your body is a
manifestation of now. It doesn't actually exist in space
or time. It exists in and as *You* in the now.

Day Two

"Enlighten your sense of self as to What You Are!"

Intimacy is a Call of Union in Being

Q: *I have been so touched in how you are speaking about sexuality and there is a profound yearning for a sexual relationship that is mature.*

B: Then, if it truly is, it won't be a sexual relationship. Intimacy is not 'sexual relationship'. Intimacy is a call of union in Being. In this, one's attention is not towards sexuality as being separate from what called you to meet another. Otherwise, if you think it is 'sexual intimacy' you will have an agenda, so you will need sex. If it is an intimate call of your being, sex won't enter the arena, only the sweetness you are discovering in Being together.

In the sweetness of discovering Being together, power or pure sexuality will move. It moves towards the attention you are in your being, or the attention you are giving to your self. It is exactly how the manifest universe is working right now.

From No-where or Awareness, light emerges. It is the light of Awareness. Some call it the Self. It is 'I', 'I' who am listening to these words right now. Then, without any split or duality, it splits into Consciousness and pure energy, both one with supreme intelligence. The entire cosmos arises out of that movement. Pure Energy manifests pure Consciousness and pure

Consciousness knows pure forming. There is no separate sense of self.

Whether we believe to be a man or a woman, whilst we have form and our awareness moves towards the truth of our being, pure energy fills our awareness in our body. *She* rises to fill the body with the pure Knowing of Consciousness. That is pure sexuality moving. It happens in just seeing the birds, the knowing of 'bird'... Instantly energy fills up the body and the heart, the Consciousness instantly deepens, expands and is forming. Instantly the body is full of Consciousness, full of energy or fullness.

When as Awareness your seeing and knowing matches your being, pure energy or pure sexuality fills up the body. That is the union of Consciousness and Energy. This is what in India is called Shiva and Shakti. I don't speak of it in this way so much as it tends to be conceptualised and produces too many images for those that are going beyond image.

You are not 'someone seeing' you are Consciousness seeing and knowing and aware. From where you see from, energy moves to form the seeing and knowing. *That* is sexuality.

If you are seeing and knowing from a limited sense of self and if you Awareness have not been enlightening your sense of self as to *What You Are*, then the moment is formed by past sexuality, which is the same as saying past experience. Whilst you place your attention only in the experience of yourself but you are knowing that that is a little deeper, your old ways will go wild within your body-mind awareness. Simply because where you put your attention, energy flows. We are not taught that energy is sexuality. We are so conditioned as to what sexuality is. It is the power to manifest where Awareness is coming from in each and every moment.

When Awareness, appearing as a man or woman, is responding to the deeper Knowing, then sexuality moves to the frequency of that Knowing. *She* dances it and it is pure and real. *She* fills up the entire body-mind intelligence with the Love that *She* Is.

It can happen that *She* appears to be residing at the root chakra but *She* doesn't, *She* will come up from the ground. *She*, sexuality. *She* is not a woman. *She* needs Consciousness here where he resides; *He*, Consciousness itself. She will come up and there is union and the expression of that union is the cosmos.

Q: *I meet such fear around this as I am listening...*

B: This is because you take yourself to be a particular woman. *She* is not a particular woman, *He* is not a particular man and neither are there men women. The closest you can get to point to their mystery is: pure masculine consciousness, pure feminine consciousness and that is The Self.

You have identified with this level of conditionality not realising that its condition is to form what you are being and that's it. If you are forming that you are a particular woman it is going to form in a deep way that you are just this particular woman.

Your sexuality is really your innate ability to create
what you are as a being because within you are neither a
man nor a woman, you are The Self and that even goes
deeper.

If we move up from that you are the pure Yin and Yang
and the moment you move, both masculine and
feminine power, energy and consciousness is
manifesting the universe. As that keeps flowing out
(without duality) of where It comes from, there is the
manifestation of what appears to be a man and woman.
Although this power of Love can find itself in two men
or two women.

Your fear is your need to control your energy to suit the
images you have created your self around. If your love
of the deep or your love of God is for man, then as long
as you hold on to those images, you will draw shallow
man. You have to see how ridiculous that is because
where 'I Am' there is no such thing as a shallow man.
But there is a play of it because he has judged himself
so much.

You will bring a man to you that won't stretch you
beyond your current comfort zones and if he does, you
will make sure he doesn't and if he still does, you will
make sure he doesn't do it again and if he still does, you
will really bring the animal out and have a go at eating
him. And if he still does, at some point you stop: 'What
is this man? " In that moment you will see him for
what *He* is beyond the man. *He* is your Love, *He* is
Consciousness itself.

In some way you are testing, whether you can 'stand'
within his consciousness, inside of *you* and whether you
can completely allow everything to fall away in his
company. Maybe you will reveal to him, which
is *you* inside, that he is this living possibility.

He is not really outside, he is inside. If he believes he is
outside you will help him get inside, however this
comes, because you are both over wanting and needing
this. You are called to discover what you deeply are in
the relatedness until your sexuality raises the roof and
the whole universe knows Love has just been made.
Because in the true direct making of Love, which is the
manifestation and the living of the universe, your light
of Awareness has entrance into the mystery of the
universe and into the deeply unseen.

That is what the making of Love is, embodied.
Your fear is losing your comfort zone. Who would you
be without all that 'knitting' going on? Your fear is that
you will go beyond your boundary and disappear into
Pure Consciousness. He will disappear into being nobody. Somehow there is a profundity at work, making
two One. Then you will explore what this making of
Love truly is and *What You Are*, right here, right now.
You will be lost in the new.

If you are not, levels of struggle will appear in your
sexuality, which basically means your creativity. You
won't know how to move anymore and you will seek
the past to rest your head in, but if you are truly called
you won't stay there for very long. Your fear is also that
you have been hurt by someone but you haven't actually
been hurt, you have just mistaken you to be a woman

and mistaken a man to be a man. You have not gone to the root of your calling together.

This is why in the East both Shiva and Shakti are in a ring of fire, because there is nothing but transformation happening and the unveiling of deeper realities, living and fully known between you, who are now One. It is the rarest realisation.

Q: *Thank you. This is very tender...and you have described perfectly what has been happening in these last years.*

B: Let's look *now*, let's not look in the past years. How is your sexuality moving right now as you listen?

Q: *What I am feeling is a greater rootedness opening and a coming down into the body. There is activation in the hands and particularly in the feet.*

B: That's it is it? So it's not moving all along in every cell of the body?

Q: *Yes of course!*

B: It's not really 'of course' unless you say it. Why did you choose to put it 'here' and there' and in isolated places in a controlled manner? Is it because if it came all the way through your body you would have no control anymore? Then your sexuality might fill the entire universe, because it does! When you realise this within this apparent humanness, your sexuality won't be that old stuff you have been taught. It is new energy

constantly filling up the body from the response of what
is deep. It's like a big 'Yes' to 'What Is'.

Q: *For me even to speak of this without any shame and
with ease is wonderful. It feels natural.*

B: You as a person have shame there. *She* is not lit up.
She is not moving through the walls, the ceiling, the
lights and every body. When *She* moves everyone
knows *She* moves.

As Awareness. with the light of our first intelligence,
we know that only Love is being made in the
manifestation of the universe. Everything else is a lie or
a distortion of an unenlightened mind and an
unenlightened nervous system or body.

This is not a problem. Shame must be allowed to move
through without our name on it. Guilt, without your
name on it. You judge yourself and in that you judge
another and everything remains the same, the same, the
same. Instead of creating the deep you just create the
same images.

We are still speaking about sexuality are we not?
You *know* when you have made Love, all your friends
know when you have made Love, your colleagues at
work know that you have made Love and the birds sing
that you have made Love and the sun shines that you
have made Love because that changes everything
here. Until even breathing is making Love, hearing the
birds is making Love. Until just your seeing is making
Love. You will just be a flow of the making of Love
and your body is the streaming of this Love moving.

Then you will no longer hold back in this life, which is holding back your sexuality and your consciousness, locked in past experience. In every moment your whole body will be open. Deeper levels of *Her* mystery will be revealed and deeper levels of *His* mystery will be revealed. Amongst all of that, the past is allowed to dissolve, to move and come home without any interruption. The past is no longer your guide, your guide is Pure Awareness seeing and knowing, and *that* is what you respond to.

This moves new energies, new consciousness and new power. Healing then is quite natural. You don't heal your past by doing anything with it. It heals by you being one with your being.

This Will Change How You Make Love

Q: *I am going through what you are speaking of with this man who is here with me now. Time and space is completely altered in this relating.*

B: When you are being deeply true time and space is deeply new. Yes, because it expands, it becomes more subtle, less time and more openness. Time stretches and in its stretch it becomes more timeless

Q: *So much old is falling away, old control systems, it is such a letting go.*

B: Within that discovery what are you discovering that is more subtle and more deep in your own experience?

Q: *We see each other, he looks at me and I see mySelf and I look at him and he sees himSelf.*

B: Yes, the seeing and knowing is seeing it sees and knows. You begin to rest deeply and profoundly. Everything is quietened. This will change how you make Love and how you are able to open, to give and to receive.

Less and less will it be about you as a someone, him as a someone. You will be able to make Love in what appears to be distance. Just in the seeing and knowing of his consciousness, the seeing and knowing of her light, Love is being made because the deep is moving.

Knowing Objectifying its Knowing

You believe we are listening to *him* (B), but in truth you are knowing Knowing. There is no him over here. That's a projection of the light of Knowing objectifying its Knowing. This happens naturally so that Awareness-Knowing can form its Knowing without a beginning and an end and that is the movement of the cosmos.

Day Three

*"The natural movement of breath, which is Life, is to
unveil the Deep. There is not a single breath you can
take that is not unveiling You."*

Veiled Life

We are all veiled life. We have veiled life with a name
and a personalising of experience. Yet there *are* levels
within our totality that are unveiled and shining. We as
Awareness tend to not recognise the levels that are
unveiled. They can be like trophies put on a shelf,
waiting for a rainy day or when we see someone we
particularly love, they shine.

The Body Transforms Food into Experience

This body is a strange and wonderful thing. It naturally
collects experience. If I gave you breakfast this
morning, then whatever it is that you deeply are, has
now transformed food into life experience. Your deeper
intelligence turns food into a body. No matter what kind
of food you eat, it transforms it into your embodiment,
into your body.

See the wonder of that! Most of us don't, we take this
for granted. Whatever is at the core of all this, is turning
that that you eat into a body, so that you can realise
what form is as the formless, as Awareness.

Can You Hear the Cosmos Breathe?
The Form Reality Practice

The Form is the expression of the realisation of the functionality of the universe in human form and its dynamics. To me that is in every cell of your body. Your body is a vehicle of cosmic expression communication and communion. The truth is that the cosmos is being poured out of Awareness right now. Can you hear it breathe? Literally Consciousness is breathing, it breathes out its innermost chambers and then it breathes them back in.

Light Conducts Love

What you are in the body is an immense transformative vehicle. You are evolving the universe of your experience. Within this there is unveiling, to unveil the deeper level realising. Unveiling opens up a profounder power of one's own awareness.

Awareness, you can sit deep and nothing really touches you for there is no experience that is not made of your essential nature. The light by which I know Thee is the light by which I know All. The quality of light is that it conducts Love and that it transports all that empties into the source of Love. We can see each other but will we all travel into the streaming of this intimacy?

The moment that Awareness, you and I, have a deeper seeing and knowing and we completely open to it, we stream up the stream of light that we appear to be coming down on. We realise the light of our Self

instantly. It is actually not going anywhere. We realise
and we are unveiled.

The Immediacy of Knowing I Am

When you are knowing anything, any *thing*, your mind
objectifies that as if you are knowing 'something'. That
seems to give this world value. In awakening, when
Knowing knows an object, the object mirrors the
knower and there is an immediacy of Knowing that has
nothing to do with the object, other than that it is a
mirror. Until all objects fail to mirror Knowing to you.
The moment you know, you know 'I Am'. You no
longer need an objective experience to tell you the
meaning of being alive.

I Am the light that is streaming the moment of
Knowing. On this level Knowing naturally arises with
phenomenal forms. They naturally arise. And within
naturally arising phenomenal forms, Awareness is
timelessly spacious and the forms do not have positive
or negative charge. They are pure forms of Awareness.
There is no polarity within them.

You Are Beyond Polarity

Awareness, as you awaken, truly awaken, you depolarise forms of experience. There is no need for you
to move by positives and negatives. In that moment you
are Pure Being moving. You have taken the 'charge' out
of these forms. If you make experiences polaric, good,
bad, right or wrong, you create someone that is

happening to. You are not someone. You are wonderfully the Only One.

You Cannot Take Your Name into the Deep

Q: I have had lots of awakening or spiritual experiences, but the realisations are not lasting in my experience.

B: When we are really clear about What I Am, this 'I', we begin to discover that it is not someone's collected thoughts and images and experiences that goes down into the deep. Our name is just a bunch of collected phenomena. It is rather like the collection of stickers or marbles that you might have had as a child

Our name is a huge magnet. Half of this magnet is polarised into one direction to collect experience, the other half is pushing it away. Basically this is what our name does, polarise experience. Unless your name is a vibration of deeper meaning. For instance, if you had a spiritual name and you were truly living its meaning, we probably wouldn't have this conversation. When you are given a name that has profound meaning, you must keep your attention within that profundity. All that you will then attract is to transform all your experience into a meaning of that name.

I have no doubt that you have had experience. It would be more correct to say: 'As Awareness I awoke to deeper dimensions of my being.' You cannot take your name to those dimensions. The moment you pass through the gate, your name cannot go through unless you have been living the meaning of your name. Then it can go through. In that manner, no one ever had the realisations.

The realisations you as Awareness have had, would have burnt away levels of your sense of self and person that were ready for immediate transformation and the streaming of you as a being up to the surface was complete. Then at some point without warning it all seemed to close. It was as if God suddenly shut the door.

Many realisers, although it is a paradox after what I just said, experience this in a similar manner. You have now come up to a level of self and person that doesn't have a relationship with you as Being. These levels were untouched by that that you were realising. Now you are asked to live in this sense of self and person and in this world, what was living in you as Awareness; its meaning, its depth, its movement, its beingness. You are asked to *live it*, up in the sense of self, body and person but free of the sense of self, body and person. The living of Love is to *now* take your realisation livingly into the corners of your sense of self and realisation. Please hear, I am not speaking about 'somebody' doing this.

In realising whatever your Awareness awoke to, you never come upon your name. You were living opened Awareness, already complete and untouched by experience. Then as Awareness, you come up into the conditional forming of experience. Through you, the deeper level can now have form and functionality as a whole being. It doesn't know any polarity, only you do on this level. Sit deeper in what you have realised and any contact with that that doesn't match the realisation will begin to vibrate. It vibrates at the energy and frequency that you put together as an image of you.

You depolarise the forms that are returning or emptying, by remaining open to where you *now* come from. The conditional level will ravage you. That is self-transformation. If you can sit open, laugh, smile, be still and you not give it any answer other than openness, you will realise that someone called by your name did not realise anything and only someone called by your name can ever experience polarities.

Awareness free of a name is Freedom itself, able to move amongst beings that are not clear who they are and see into all the possibilities that actually exist in this cosmos.

The Past is Now

You can only speak of *now*. Use your mind and you will be speaking of the past. But the past is *now*, it is in the *now*.

When you see this, you can't be bothered to speak about the past. It was always *now*, made of the *now*, but coloured. Now you love the light itself, you are longer bothered by the colours of the past. You love the full presence of 'What Is' and the past is washed and you land in what *now* really is. It is *now* that you move, *now* that you are still, *now* that you are capable as the *now*. It is *now* that you have the capacity, as *now*, to move the universe of your life, one with the deeper communion of what you deeply first are.

You lovingly and with full care do not step away from this. If you do, you usher yourself back like you would usher a butterfly out of a closed room, so that it can fly in the spaciousness of what it is.

You Want It All

You want it *All*, but if you want it *All*, It has to live you and you have to live what *It* is up on the surface. That is a pure state of openness.

Your Deepest Longing

Do you know what your deepest longing is? When you get to a certain level of awakening, your deepest longing is for everyone you meet to be free. Your heart hurts because you want everyone to be free, you want to exchange in Love and beauty and wonder.

But then you are going to have to be one with each other's experience. You cannot say that is someone else's experience over there. You must go into it, enter it with them and experience it, not foolishly but with a flaming heart. You are willing to burn too, impersonally. I burn for you constantly, because I love you so deep in this Love that we are.

A Matrix of Connectivity

Your nervous system is rather like the Ley lines on planet earth. If you go any deeper you will realise Ley lines within the cosmos. Science calls them a gravitational grid. They are the matrix of connectivity. It might seem like we are separate and sitting in different places, but your mind, which is really the mind of God, manifests the brain through your Awareness. The brain is not an individuated brain. Your brain turns perception into sense-perception. It looks like you have a brain that is yours, but you could say there is a big brain here in the human psyche. It is of cosmic proportions and it is wired in to the whole matrix of the cosmos. It is singularly wired into the deep.

It looks like you are 'someone', having to deal with an overload of information in your nervous system. That overload of too much information is the totality of thoughts and feelings since this so called humanness began. All the information since life on the planet first moved. A storehouse of experience but no one's in particular. Just the true story of the evolution of man-woman-kind.

All that information is in the nervous system. To a much larger degree, in a finer deeper place, the evolution of all beings in the cosmos is available. Whilst you think you are a someone it will blow your circuitry. It will be too much power for you to bring through what you believe is you. Isn't it amazing that the 'I' that begins it all, the 'I' that ends it all and the 'I 'that begins it all and ends it all again, is *here now*, appearing as you and I?

And as the 'I' having access to: 'I know I Am that I Am'? The moment you are able to respond to this Knowing is called 'awakening'. Then you are responding to and realising more of what you deeply are in the unseen, appearing in the cosmos. You realise: 'I Am That that creates, I Am That that dissolves, I Am That that is knowing the deep and, without doing anything, is forming the universe. I Am that I Am.'

The Only Answer

The one who is listening is the only answer to everything that takes place. If that one makes its domain in thoughts and feelings of a linear nature, then you are not the answer but you are the problem. Your self becomes the problem; *You* identified with your self. When you don't identify with your self you are *You*. Who are You? What are You? Ask this before you speak a single word. You are aware. You are knowingly aware. Always go with what is *first* first and not last. Thoughts and feelings are last.

You Are Not on Your Own

Whilst you have separated *What You Are* from your self and person, you will think you are someone who is dealing with life on your own.

When you are really open, your nervous system and
everyone's nervous system within this field, is taking
through self-transformation. You are not dealing with
what you thought you were dealing with on your own.
And you are not awakening as somebody awakening.
You become the awakening of the One in a field of
Oneness, able to realise the deep and move that in the
nervous system, whilst transforming in an instant, the
self-images in this field of humanness. You are not on
your own, but you could say that humanness is one
humanity.

There is a much speedier transformation within a group
field, of people who are given to not holding back and
remaining open, no matter what. Then what is conveyed
deeply moves through the field. The possibility to
transform each form within this field of Beingness is at
its highest. Then there is not your nervous system and
someone else's, not your realisation and someone else's,
it is the One realising itself, transcending
itself transforming itself and moving itself and living
possibility is the movement of Love. Conversations like
this encourage each and every one of us to be so open
within our experience. Then there is a recognition of the
same or familiar experiences, for in essence we are the
same one with a little wonderful difference.

Then we don't have to sit tightly on our chairs, we
might find ourselves on the edge of our seats in awe and
wonder of all this and its capacity to heal, to make real,
to deepen, to open, to reveal. This is of benefit to all
beings.

Fulfilment

When we relate to the deeper knowing of our aware
experience our awareness expands, deepens and there is
more aliveness. We transcended this idea that our
personalising experience fulfils us. We realise that
fulfilment is within our being. Then we can move
together as fulfilled beings. That will deepen and the
field is transcending, growing and the light of
Awareness is shining through each body-mind.
We are the same One, no longer divided.

Day Four

*"Everything speaks the language of the Beloved
when you look deep enough."*

Perception Changes in Deeper Belonging

This moment of existence is being streamed by you as
Awareness. When the body drops away you will move
in that stream and you will be very aware of that
streaming. You will move in that stream as Awareness
to wherever you are returning to. No matter where you
move to, you will still be Awareness and you will still
be knowingly aware that you are knowingly aware.

We know everything that we know in our familiar sense
through the light of Knowing but that light of Knowing
has been objectified. When we cease objectifying the
Knowing there is immediate opening, communing and
communication of the deeper Knowing. There is no one
'over there' and when the same light that you see each
other with, meets the same streaming, the deep opens up
in your hearts and you begin to experience the opening
of what is deeper than the familiar and the known. In
that moment you are a body of joy, but that joy is
beyond the word 'body' and the miracle or the wonder
of it is that you transcend the body mind and yet it is
included. You are actually in another place, other than
human experience. The human experience opens up to
the extraordinary experience of 'I am Aware' and an
immediate power of Pure Being opens.

You know you are in a different place and yet all the
senses stream that place as the birds, the bees, the trees

the mountains, the people. You begin to see that perception changes in deeper Belonging. You see everything for what it is, meaningfully, deeply, wholly, really. Sense perception itself is the movement of light, the same light by which we know, see and are together. As Awareness realises deeper and responds to that deepening, that deepening manifests here, without any doing. Nobody did it. It is the belonging to the deeper opening that brings it here. It changes the mind and the body. It changes everything because it is an awakening to a deeper dimension, not a dimension of change, but a dimension of wholeness. One knows one is whole.

In being wholly one with that deeper Knowing, the brain opens in areas of the brain that are not yet opened. It is scientifically known that humans only use a small percentage of their brain. The deeper levels of the brain are inaccessible to the familiar sense of consciousness. They will only open to the higher frequencies of a living being. It is as though we are protected from our own depth because our depth will destroy our make-believe reality.

Pain And Turmoil Have Made You More Open to Receive 'What Is'

If you look at this openly, everything in your life particularly pain, particularly turmoil, the broken dreams, the failed desire, the failed partnerships have made you more open to receive what truly is. Now the door is open but only the unfamiliar can be, see, know and have. Because what is deeper must have everything and it knows no past. We are all sitting together because to some degree we are giving up the pictures of our past by entering their shadows awake, even though that can be devastating to who we believed we were.

It is a preparation for extraordinary Awareness to awaken and deeper possibilities to live, for your beingness to give expression to the deep.

Ask yourself, has or is pain pointing you with a clear arrow into the deep? What has it shown you? Is it showing you how to be clear and whole or does it show you to rely on the past and function from past experience? Are you allowing the past to burn? Simply because you are not using it anymore. If pain is an arrow to the deep, there will be moments of indescribable fear that just happen. Suddenly there is panic from nowhere, fear blown out of all proportion.

Then there are moments of doubts that you didn't even know were still there but now they are amplified. These are all signs of deeper awakening. They are the clearing within the psychic system, the nervous system, the body-mind of the reliance of 'what was' and not what truly is, because the 'Is' transcends all worlds and then is available to move through all of them; Pure Living Awareness.

Do You Need More False Experience?

Are you seeing that arrow of pain? Do you need more pain? Do you need more false experience to know you are pure experience? Pure Awareness knowingly

aware, that, that the entire cosmos arises in and dissolves in. Are you realising *What You Are*?
Yes? Then begin to see how it has instant relationship in 'What Is'.

It All Heads Back to its Source, Which is Now

In awakening you will disturb your own mind with the shocking truth that it is all *You*. You will disturb your entire nervous system of all the pictures you have put into it. You keep looking into these pictures to see that you are getting it right. They are all nicely tucked into your sleepy nervous system. Waking up is that all those images and sensations wake up in *You* Awareness. It all begins to head back to its source. You will believe there is an army on the march but they are all your children on their way home, which is *now*.

Knowing Has No Form

When you know that that is deeper, it has no form or experience other than 'Knowing'. When Awareness, appearing as you and I, wholeheartedly says: "Yes!" to Knowing, the truth of that Knowing moves. You know its movement. It is both thrilling and stilling, it is clear and it is whole. It is Love, instantly filling up your heart and entire body.

You learn without learning in all the mishaps, in all the ups and downs, in all the failures, in all that you wanted to happen and it never did. In the crash of all your beliefs you remember the movement as Being, not moving in the pictures but moving as a being of the beyond. It is a placeless place. The place to which you return in deep dreamless sleep.

Now you no longer listen to any other news, but the news that there is only one Good moving, one Good breathing, one Good living. You begin to discover your whole beingness and it is only ever discovered in *this* moment.

A picture, a sensation or an old energy will surely come and is made really believable in the body. The body makes real everything you believe and your first old belief that will fail is this one: "But I *feel* this is right!" That one will crash. The very core of feeling will empty out because not until Being touches on the core of feeling, will you know the feeling of
Love, which is not a feeling.

You will become more silent in the movement of your humanness. You are no longer listening to the body-mind brain box idea of who you are. All those old ideas will come to meet you from inside and outside, from friends, family, politicians. You will be letting go of all this, until all that you respond to is the depth of your Knowing. Then it moves *as you* and up into the body. This it is *living* Truth, then your entire body registers the deep.

Profoundly In It Profoundly Beyond It

Enter this life fully, don't turn away because you come on the edge of your identification with the sense of self. You have come upon what we are speaking of here so many times and then you fall for the idea of being a 'someone'.

You don't have attention deficit. You choose to give your attention to your sense of self. It seems valuable to you until you really realise it is not giving you anything other than perfect failure! It is so simple to arrive in perfect failure. You begin to get it, you begin to get that you are still living, still alive and somehow you are even more aware and more available for life as it is. You don't have to make-believe anything anymore. You don't have to go and get it. It is unfolding and you have access into the deep.

Then your failures may come to you through others, you will hear your stories through other people and you will hear your stories through the newspaper and through the media. You have to hear it everywhere. That way what you are awakening as, integrates everywhere. You will see a miracle of Love taking place, an intelligence that is 'what it is' no matter what. It is moving, living, evolving the universe. It is fully involved in it this power of 'I', and it is I who am listening to these words now. Profoundly beyond it, profoundly in it; Non-Duality!

Form is not Limited

Form is only as limited as you are aware *in* it. The body-mind or form is only as limited as how you limit your own Awareness. It is only as limited as you will remain identified with wanting and needing. Awareness believes it is contained within a form of experience and not that the form of experience is contained *in* Awareness.

When you hear this, there is growth and depth and the building of a higher self. In other words your intelligence climbs a few ladders. Your energy isn't confined just to 'below the belt', so you are not controlling your formed experiences. Awareness, Consciousness and energy go beyond the roof, you are all open.

Form is not limited in that it is made of Awareness. When Awareness truly becomes aware that the light of Knowing is its true Self, you transcend form and then include it quite naturally. You are only capable of what is beyond form *in* form when your Awareness is clearly responding to the deep. Then it is not just *your*

Awareness that expands but all the forms of Awareness grow. If you are limited so are your forms.

When Awareness responds to the deep, that is the making of true form, in an instant. True form is the pouring of the formless, instantly creating form. Those forms are real forms, they don't have anybody's name on them. They are not imagined. It is the movement of Pure Being manifest.

On Fear

Nothing that is real can ever be afraid of anything. Fear is the relationship between Awareness identified with self, and the imagined experiences in a seeming past. The moment Awareness looks into the past, it looks into pictures and energies seemingly in the past. The moment you identify with any image, the seeming gap between what you deeply know and that image creates fear.

When Awareness doesn't relate to the past, it has no image of 'What Is', so there is no limiting sense of self that has sprung up from an imagined past. In such bright Awareness there is no fear. Have a relationship with your self and you will have fear. Deeply relate to *What You Are* and your self will build in the likeness of your relationship with the deep. All that can fear are the speaking images of your past. Don't listen to them. It is not *you*. Those images and their energy will dissolve by you no longer having anything to do with them.

Look at the past, relate to the past and you will have fear in the present. Remain true to what is deeper and you will be presence, you won't have fear. Only identity as a self will have fear. It is not that you are dissolving your fear, you are letting go of this body-mind idea that you are a 'someone'.

Everything is interconnected in the all-ness, in the Oneness, in the deep. Right now Awareness is registering the deep and the manifest and the Knower of that is the one who is listening to these words now.

There is nothing to do other than to let the registration happen. As you truly become open, Awareness naturally responds to the deep. There are no longer reactions on the surface. Your response to the deep and your response to the manifest becomes equal, because you *are* the One on both apparent levels. *You* are equal and everything is arriving in 'equal-ness'. There is no positive and negative in the equal-ness of your Awareness. Bad is as equal as good. It is all made of that One. The living of this is enlightened Awareness in its fullest.

Attention Led by Thought

Unless you are attentive to this moment, you will be on the lead of our mind leading you to all manner of concerns. Concerns about you, your family or about what is going on in the world. All those concerns are the manifestation of thinking.

It is clear that you cannot *think* about Now. Thought is a past image. It leads you to the past and the same thought then leads you towards the future to get rid of that thought. Your attention led by thought always lands your attention in what *was*, what *should be* or what *could be*. Your thought gives you a centre and in truth you have no centre. You are Pure Awareness, in which every form and all experience arises. You build a centre by following a thought.

As Awareness, if you keep your attention completely Now, every thought will come to your attention, instead of your attention going to every thought. Thinking makes you believe you have a centre and then you will centre your attention on images. Learn to be open where all that lives as you, Pure Awareness.

Your mind will tell you: "I need to sort things out," but they don't resolve in a deep meaningful way when you have a centre! You will be self-centred about everything. You won't be available to be open to it *all*. When you as Awareness are present you won't be functioning as a thought, you will be the movement of openness, able to hear, able to feel, able to see and move without a centre. You will be knowing wholeness. You will be wholly present with those you are with.

The moment you think, there is conflict in you because thought gives you a self-centre and an objective past. This disturbs your moment of being present. Now you are encoded with thought that has a feeling. Basically you end up chasing pictures and that leads to more conflict.

When we see that we cannot think about Now, that is
the end of self-concern. There will be pure openness,
which manifests as relaxation in the body, clarity in the
mind and as a heart that is enabled to speak and hold *all*
in Love. The very attention of being a self-centre now
integrates into the body and the body opens to its deeper
mystery. There is only presence living this
moment. This is not a concept, but we each have to
discover this.

What we love is that we are the same openness. Only
thought is conflicting between us. openness has no
means of conflict. Openness that has no past or future is
pure creation; Now. You can reach into openness and
into the openness of an apparent other. There is pure
sensation, pure energy, ecstatic presence or simple
delightful openness. There is no one who does not yearn
for that simplicity. It is obscured by a self-centre that is
just an idea of thinking.

Crisis Points You to the Real

If you are listening to this, it means you are in crisis.
The crisis is that you have gone beyond your familiar
model of yourself. You have gone beyond what you
once believed you were and there is nothing in your life
or in your self that fits what you are awakening to.

You are in crisis because you are awakening beyond
your familiar sense of self. That crisis shows up in your
nervous system when you act from the past. The body-
mind registers the crisis, in that what is now available is

more than what is programmed or patterned into the
body-mind.

Most people don't recognise they are in crisis. I am
speaking here of those that believe they are awakening.
Because you have to see you are awakening to what is
profoundly deeper than how you are living your life. I
am speaking of the *manner* in which you are living
here, not the forms necessarily, although the forms
aren't matching the frequency of what you as
Awareness are awakening to.

The moment that you do anything, that crisis shows up
in your nervous system and in how you relate. You are
pulled to Truth and yet you are living less than what
you are pulled to. You try to sort your life out by
mixing what you are knowing deeper with the forms
you move in. It doesn't work.

That is the crisis one enters when one truly awakens.
You cannot give yourself to the old model, the old way
anymore. You are called to be deeply true. You don't
know how this will look, but you do know that it is
what you love, so you find the way. The way isn't in all
the appearance of things. The way is how you find the
inner way in all that appears to be outer. You will still
come upon crisis until you no longer fear it. You
become quite courageous. If things need to change they
change. You go with the consciousness of that change
and you constantly find the new deeper way. Otherwise
you just remain in crisis, functioning from old belief-
systems that you have actually gone beyond. You are
diving deep and you are letting this deep-dive change
the surface.

You are not changing the surface, you are being deeply
true to the deeper level you are awakening to. This will
change the surface forms that you used to relate to, as
showing you *What You Are.*

In trying to handle or manipulate those surface forms,
you enter a deeper crisis, until the crisis shakes you free
of the absurdity of believing that the surface could ever
speak for you, act for you or *be* you. Then you move in
a deeper manner, by being one with Truth.

Forms on the surface continue to change but now they
they are true forms of what you are deeply awakening
to. You no longer need form to tell you *What You Are.*
You are Awareness awakening, one with the deeper
truth of the light of your Real Self. Can you hear this?

Truth doesn't give you any hope. Truth doesn't give
you a rope. Truth simply makes you naked and not need
anything to be deeply true to. Your immediate guide is
being true. Until you are simply Being Truth. Crisis is
pointing to the new, the real. Reality itself, meaning
itself. It deeply is what *You* first are.

Where does this touch you? It will resonate, strike cords
within, and it will be registered up on the surface. You
will recognise the crisis. You just haven't seen it as a
crisis. It is a crisis of belonging and belief.

Have you ever seen an abandoned town or city? Where
I live, whole suburbs were abandoned because of
earthquakes and seismic activity. You can see rows of
houses with trees growing through the windows,
completely abandoned. No one lives there anymore.

This is rather like leaving your old ways behind. You have to realise you don't live there anymore. Really see you do not live there anymore, so that nature can take over the old buildings. You are like the abandoned town, you don't live there anymore. I am giving you this as an image that you can translate into the abandonment of your old way. It is a powerful image but it is beyond imagination.

In the crisis it is unimaginable to abandon your old way. In the crisis your old way is coming up through every crevice. The old abandoned town comes up in every possible way; in the newspapers, on the radio, in your old favourite songs, old favourite books, your friends, your family. It comes in every way.

Will you be clear "I do not live there anymore"? You have to announce this with every fibre of your body. You will be accused of being insensitive but you are actually becoming acutely sensitive. A speck of dust could cry and you would know it. This is how open you are becoming. Most would not go this way. Most don't want to recognise this crisis. But the crisis of Consciousness awakening to the truth of its own Pure Being is real and it is demonstrable in life.

Begin to whole-heartedly say that you do not live there anymore. You are discovering living what is beyond, like a baby you are learning to walk the beyond. You are learning to speak the 'beyond language'. You have no interest in your old way. It makes no difference that this makes you unrecognisable to most people. Love recognises its own. Do you recognise the crisis in a real way? If you don't, it simply continues the suffering of a split apprehension of things. *You* want to dive into what Reality is, which is your deepest nature and calling.

Would you let go of everything to dive deeper without needing to know how that is going to look? Tell me, what will death look like? You don't know. Does it have you opening? Then you are already well through the crisis. Does it have you closing? Then you are holding onto some belief that you need something of the past to relate to. All you need is knowing *What You Are*. Present Knowing-Aware; unspeakable and yet it speaks in everything. Inexpressible and yet it forms and forms are animated by what it is. It is the one listening to these words now.

The Search for More Experience Ends

As you truly awaken you won't be making or searching for more experience. You won't find much experience of *having* or *doing* something. It no longer gives you a sense of Beingness, so you will stop reaching for more.

And you naturally let go of the forms that used to give you experience, they dissolve. You become quieter and quieter inside. The Love, the Truth you awakened to, you realise *is You*. Your need of any other experience falls away and you courageously explore *What You Are,* what this 'I' of Knowing points into.

You leave all your old ways behind. Tenderly and utterly vulnerably you find the way that matches your deepest Knowing. You recognise it intimately, deeply.

It no longer matters to you what comes and goes. What now matters is what never comes and never goes, but what remains. You experience Awareness knowingly aware.

In your love of Truth you enter *What You Are*. Not only does that dissolve old forms on the surface, but true forms move. It no longer matters to you whether it is a true form or a false form. You are coming alive in meaning.

Questions Disappear

Q:I feel as though every question and answer has disappeared and also the necessity for either.

B: The question and answer may disappear for a moment. Then the question of life, of "How shall I live?" arises. Because there is movement of life, through an apparent 'other' or a need of activity, such as that you will be making your food, walking down the street, looking after the children. Whatever you do, there is going to be activity. You will be aware of that activity and you will be *in* it. The activity relates or reflects to you: "What are you?".

Someone will speak to you, how will you answer? As if you are someone they know and they are someone you know? Immediately you are called to answer the question: "Where do you come from? What do you know? What are you?"
It is a question is it not? It is the only constant here. In its movement it is Love, in its depth, Truth.

How will you answer? Action *is*. It looks like people are doing the action but movement is the action of Consciousness. Within that movement, Consciousness discovers what *It Is* or what it is not. It realises within the action What I Am, or it simply relates to the body-mind and its activity: "I am a man, I am a woman, I am an office worker, I am a scientist"….But is that the truth? Do you not long to live as Truth? Then you must discover *What You Are* in *all* activity.

Action or activity questions *What You Are*. Yes, the question and answer may fall away, such as in deep dreamless sleep. Apparently you wake up in the morning, then how shall you live? You don't ask yourself this because you just live everyone else's life. You will live all the conditional forms, the conditional forms of your society, your education, your google search. You live through all this shallow stuff and all that is ok to be there, but will you live the *more* within your google search?

To know *What You Are* and be *What You Are* is always the question of daylight, until there is no night and day for you. It is realised that Awareness does not sleep, ever. So each moment is a question. "What am I, Who am I? How shall I live?" The planet itself has come to this crisis of identity. This is always the question until you are living as Awareness because that is what you deeply are.

There will still be questions. "Would you like tea or cappuccino?" "What time shall I get up in the morning?" "Don't forget to pick up the children." "Will you take me to the station? "Wonderful, ordinary life still moves but the question of Reality itself exists. It will never cease. "Who am I? What am I?" is the question of each breath.

When you really get this, the body completely relaxes. All the tension within the body, is through not answering that question. In being the living answer everything relaxes deeper and deeper. You are the question and the answer and it all simply unfolds. You get caught in the headlights of the amazement of what you are seeing and knowing. The headlights begin to relax, everything goes completely deeply black and you soften into the deep and you wonderfully lose all self-centredness just like in deep dreamless sleep. Then the light comes on. The light is the question of life, its movement, its brightness, its living and its return.

Going Home

It is not long before you will all be going home. Outwardly you know where that is. How will you know it inwardly? You do. If you respond to Knowing, the inward way home, the delight of being open is the experience of Being Knowing Aware.

You know when you enter your heart. You know when you enter and you know when you don't fully enter. You know that you know you know. It is a trinity. You have to complete the trinity. You know you know you know.

Stay knowingly at the door of the heart until it opens. Only then will you know what the heart is. You will discover that is the first door into *What You Are*. Then go and find out what is next. What is deeper than the heart? The moment you know you know you know opens the door. Now you can walk in. Keep walking in.

Day Five

*"All your intimacies come to a single intimacy.
That intimacy is the realisation of Love and the
realisation that Love moves from Truth."*

Relate From and As The Deep

Remain in and respond to the deep. This is the same as
saying: address and relate to this life, to your intimate
partner, your family, your friends from and as the depth
amongst all the conditioned concepts of how you should
act, behave and move. This movement of depth which is
moving *now* as light transforms the sense of self and
you experience a match of Being up in the level of your
self.

You discover that there is nothing but intimacy here. It
seems like that kind of intimacy threatens your known
familiar sense of self. Threatened with so much
intimacy one may experience a contraction inside.
Maybe one, maybe two, maybe several but the
contraction is 'holding' this moment of experience and
discovering 'What It Is', like a meditation or
contemplation. The contraction is a door to a deeper
interior, although the mind might go crazy, the emotions
might be chaotic, there is an initiation into a deeper
door of reality.

Deeper reality cannot come up into form that is not as
open. The known cannot mix with the unknown. The
raising up of the self, the opening of mind beyond
concept, is the un-mixing. Something real is taking

place. You may want to move away from that but you will return. The body-mind is designed to, at some point, completely open for it is made of light, the light of Awareness.

Resistance

What is resistance? Is there anyone resisting or is that another illusion? Is resistance the meeting of form that doesn't match the deeper awakening? Form that doesn't match the frequency of the freedom you know inherent in Being. Invent someone who exists, that is ignorance. There is no one resisting, there is just 'resistance'. Resistance is like making a form more smooth. It is like sandpaper. It is not that you want to experience a smoother life, it the natural endeavour for forms of experience to match your knowing of Awareness, to match your being. There is no one resisting. That's like saying there is no one perceiving, there is only 'perception'. But then in an instant, perception can seem to be known by 'someone' in this magical mystery individualising the wholeness. It is God or Source awakening to itself as each and every one of us.

Resistance is a level of experience up in the self and person that doesn't match the deepening and widening of Awareness knowing it knows. You are used to translating that as: "I have resistance, I have a problem, it is called my partner or my family, my work, my self and he or she or they feel like sandpaper to me."

As Awareness you are endeavouring to come up into this level of reality which is *you*, for the listener *is* the

one and only Reality behind all experience. You are
endeavouring to come up into this form and for your
form of experience to match the Knowing of the
awakening in the deep but you must enter and go right
into the forms of any experience, awake!

Human intelligence has tried to make all the roughness
and hardness more bearable. So you keep seeking
comfort but the roughness and hardness is the nature
that points to *What You Are*. It only becomes finer or
smooth by you fully entering the roughness, the cutting,
the burning. Somehow it all works miracles.

Form is the Word

When as Awareness you voice the Knowing,
it is formed.

Form isn't necessarily solid.

Form is the word; the word: "I know I know" forming.
All *this* is made of light, the light of Knowing.

The Living Forming of the Beyond

As Awareness heartfully softens it flows and expands
beyond the concept of form, beyond any notion that
there was ever matter here. It is all made of the light of
Awareness. This becomes a living experience of
fullness and possibility. You won't know death. You are
already the living forming of the beyond as you live this
awakening.

Sexuality Matches the Movement of Being

Within this apparent human experience, sexuality matches the movement of being true to Being. Notice how in your mind you are keeping sexuality down in the root chakra, because that is the only place you are going to control experience. If this energy rises above the navel, there is no longer any control of the experience of energy or sexuality.

The ability to give expression to What I Am is through pure energy or sexuality moved *as one* with the Beingness 'I Am', communing and communicating. You experience this communication as the full embodiment of Being Now. When Awareness (you and I) is true to Knowing or Being, sexuality or pure energy is the embodiment of Pure Being. This is the cosmic body.

Sexuality then is no longer condemned to the lower survival centre, it is moved into total expression of the divine. This is what is actually here, appearing as the cosmos. The dance of this is manifesting the divine.

When we then speak together we don't confine energy or Consciousness to survival. Within this openness the embodiment of the divine or the pure is not in some hoped-for future, it is communed, moved and made real Now. Your whole body hears, knows and expresses Truth.

The moment Awareness, up on the level of body, self and person is true to the core of Being, the very energy that makes creation possible moves in alignment with the truth of Being. Responding to Being moves energy to manifest what Being is in form.

Within any moment, which *is* Now, that you apprehend deeper Knowing and it has all your attention, this deeper Knowing streams as a movement in your body. The body then is an emergence of the deep or the unseen. Now, when you speak to another there is a conveyance of that emergence of Being knowing forming. It is always Now. In that moment you are knowing the embodiment of what you know to be true and it is *You*.

It has nothing to do with sex. With intimacy? Oh yes! Embodied? Oh yes! The moment of embodiment *is* the expression of the deeper. There is flowering within the Consciousness and flowering within the body. It is a garden! You realise there is no separation.

Crete Retreat

*"Within the retreat our true, open, heartfelt enquiry
will constantly be, not 'Who am I?'
but 'What am I?'
and from there only know the self,
this human self that seems to be the heart
of our problem and our difficulty."*

Opening Night

*"Gatherings like this make so much more possible.
The smallest calling that we know within,
without knowing what it is,
can flower and have life in such a group.
Your heart is already in response to a much
deeper, clearer orientation in your life."*

You Called Everyone to Be Here

Do you realise the kind of energy you have brought?
You have brought tremendous energy with you to this
retreat and if there is any fear in you, it is not of *him*
(B), it is of *You*. It is the fear of this tremendous energy
and power, which is masked by our belief that we are
someone that can do right or wrong, good or bad, when
in truth everyone is looking for their own light in all
these wonderful mirrors. Have a look around at these
wonderful mirrors.

Realise that *You* called everyone on this retreat to be on
this retreat. You called everyone here, you have called
each other. When you look at someone's face your brain
configures the face as if you have met them before on
the surface but the deep ignores that impression and
pulls you to know them in the *new* that they have
entered.

You are not the same one. I will not discuss the past
with you. You are not the same one. You are a new one.
You are different. It is not that you did anything to

make yourself different. It is just how it happens. You are all different. Welcome!

I look at you and I see such wonder. Have a look around at this wonder called 'us'. Let us all use this moment right at this beginning, to breathe in the power of this openness that is *here*, in all of us.

The Deep Waved

Last night there were some huge waves here, the deep was coming up and it waved. It thundered and lightning shot across the sky. I would say that your life has been rather like that storm for you to have been able to even arrive here.

Your New Nervous System

The human nervous system can handle so much more than we believe. You are all sitting in a field of bright potential. Your mind won't know about it, but your heart does. Your heart is picking it up. *You* are picking up this connection.

When you look at each other, when you glance around the room, know that 'All This' is your new nervous system. This is the nervous system that you have always wanted. This is your new nervous system for you to be able to put through so much more of the deeper realising of what your essential nature is. Truly look at it! Stay open. Your eyes are changing. You have a greater capacity to see from within. There is no one standing on their own, all alone. There is only the vastness of this light of Awareness shining right now. Everyone, wherever you are looking from, *this* is your bigger body. This is why we gather. We gather to build a bigger body to realise the brighter body of Awareness.

Day One

*"The light of What You Are is longing
to realise what It is. It's the only constant here.
I call this 'The Calling'."*

I Am That I Am

As we truly soften, the knowing 'I Am' deepens. It
doesn't go into relating. It doesn't move into objective
experience, such as thought, feeling or memory. It is the
pure, absolute recognition: 'I Am'.

It is clear, 'I Am That I Am'. There is no colouring of
experience, it is non-relative. Discover the truth of this
'I Am that I Am'. Even within this non-relative
objective nature it is a shining brightness.

I close my eyes and there is a shining brightness in the
blackness of: 'I am aware'. I open my eyes and there is
a shining brightness appearing as life itself functioning,
moving, living. It is still non-relative, not relating; a
flow of the light of What I Am, having function without
relationship. No mind, no body, not someone, not two.
Yet it is having dancing forms of life and a functionality
that is not based on individuality or separateness.

With your eyes closed, in the recognition of this non-
relative functionality, notice there is softness in the
openness of 'I Am' and the 'I' points beyond itself
as an 'I'.

Up on the level of embodiment, as Awareness comes up

in the 'I Am', there is softness and openness. There may
be energy and sensation but the ground of it is one's
own pure being.

There is still no function in terms of *relative* but the
functionality is simple and often missed: we are
exploring Consciousness itself. All this is an
exploration of conscious Awareness.

Clearly I am aware 'I Am' and I *know* I am aware.
There is openness, clarity and there is a biological,
metaphysical movement up on the surface. The heart is
beating. It is clear to you that the body is being lived.
The body is *Being lived*, but is there a body?

Open your eyes and you are still in the knowing 'I Am'
and you are seeing clearly that on the outside (until you
discover there is no such thing as an outside) the
cosmos, the universe, the body is moved in
functionality. It has function. 'I' is a living expression
of Being. Really look at this, there is no one looking at
it as a 'someone' but there is Being Knowing Aware,
for I Am That I Am.

Waking Up in The Morning

In waking up in the morning there is a moment of Pure
Being that is non-doing and yet there is a vibrant
functionality; the body is living, the birds are singing,
the sun is shining. On the outside everything is
functioning or is it *Being lived*?

As Awareness knowing 'I Am', to speak of 'waking up'

in the morning actually makes no sense. It makes no sense from this place! There is no waking up, there is only Awareness knowing 'I Am'.

Then there is an impulse to get up; 'I Am knowingly aware I Am' gets up in the morning. As knowing Awareness moves up into the forms of experience, there is a movement of body-mind or a sense of self, this apparent individuation of I Am. "Hi Love, did you sleep well? " Up on this apparent level of 'being someone', Awareness knowingly aware has entered a streaming of its own pure forming. Within the forming there seems to come an experience of colourisation of Being Aware. I now seem to be someone in the colours of yesterday and apparently I have a tomorrow, a future. It is a colour. Awareness comes up and mind speaks as if it is *you*.

One Field of Aware Knowingly Aware

As we move in this together, it is one field of attention, one field of Awareness, one field of 'Aware knowingly Aware'. Then there can be no one with an overload in their nervous system. The nervous system in the human body is the biology of Pure Awareness; pure in nature, metaphysical as it builds its own expression of 'I Am'. The nervous system conducts this knowing of 'I Am' up into forms of experience that don't belong to a somebody but to the totality 'I Am that I Am'.

Discover!

Discover 'What I Am'. How deep does this Knowing go? How deep does this 'aware-ing' go? How wide and real is it? You will also discover this idea of a separate sense of self, often called 'me'...

We have gone somewhat into the true nature of Awareness in the knowing 'I Am'. There is most definitely endlessly more to go into. Endlessly!
Now we will touch on this idea of a separate sense of self that is conditional. There is no one that is not, has not, will not experience the conditional nature of a believed separate sense of self.

Thought Invents Distance and Time

Notice that thought has a distance and any distance invents time. You then have to travel in thought in time. A thought will have you looking at the past, a thought will throw you into the future and a thought will have you drop the Pure Knowing I Am. Thought will move as thought to reach a distance and relate to that distance.

Thinking is distance, thought and time. Awareness is distancing itself from what it is as 'I Am'. It is a constant mis-identification with 'What Is'.

We are taught this. Our tendency is to think about ourselves, which distances our Knowing. In truth you cannot ever be distant from *What you Are*, but you can up in your mind. You distance the form of yourself

from what you already are. By believing in a thought
you create the time that distances You from You.
It is all a mirage but that is what is happening and that
imprints in the nervous system, in the body, the heart
and in the mind as more images, more colouring and
more obscuration.

Awareness that knows 'I Am that I Am' plays the game
of moving, not as 'What It Is' in Being-ness, but it
creates a distance from its true nature. It is just a game.

The moment you think, you move by thought, which
creates time in your sense of self. The moment you
make time, you make distance and it will take you time
to travel that distance.

You know in our sense of self that it takes time to move
from one apparent place to another but it takes no time
whatsoever to be *What You Are,* and it does not require
a movement of any manner of function.

Being Streamed

Is it becoming clear to you as we sit here, that this room
is being streamed? Streamed, by 'I Am that that I Am'?
All this is arising and it is arising and having form
simply because on this level we have a brain that forms
what is arising and creates sense of the perception and
the knowing 'I Am that I Am'.

The body is actually a streaming of light and Awareness
forming in the presence of 'I Am' with no distance, no
time, no space and no objective experience, for it is

already full of what It Is.

Whilst Awareness takes hold of a thought and identifies with a thought, not knowing what a thought is, the brain turns the thought into a solid experience of 'I am someone' and right there into the conditionality of our self, since we believe we incarnated, of our family, since we believed this is our family, of our nation, since we believed we are a nation and so forth. The body-mind will make all these experiences real because of You Awareness, for it must *do* or form what you believe you are. It must.

But really this is a stream of Pure Consciousness right *now*. On this level, a formed experience of 'What Is'. Light itself is form and it carries the much needed patterning of life to make all this wonder possible in human form.

Even a tree has a being. See the tree, it appears to be physical to you up on the level of perceived physicality, but drop a little bit deeper and the tree becomes as much Being as you are. It is Being a tree. It has a metaphysical movement, a movement of light and energy made of the appearance of materialising. It is real and functional, biological, apparently physical, metaphysical mixed with patterns of a proposed past and energies of a finer sense of its being. There is so much more to 'What I Am' than just the biological, just the physical, just the mental.

The Collapse into What I Am

In our schools and in our lives we are mostly not shown or pointed in the direction of 'What I Am'. We are pointed to the *becoming*, to 'what I will become', not towards 'What I Am'.

What we are looking at here is really not very 'becoming' to our sense of self.

(B enacts a dialogue in two voices back and forth)

A: *"Oh, this is not very 'becoming'!"*

B: "That's right, it is not very becoming."

A: *"Oh, so what is this that I feel?"*

B: "It is the collapse of what you have become."

A: *"But I don't like the feeling of that! You are telling me this is what I have become? And it is collapsing and that is the feeling in my sensation, the disturbance in my heart and in my mind and that's the disturbance in my relationship with you and others, with this life and me?"*

B: "Yes. Yes!"

A: *"You mean there is no one else that is causing this?"*

B: "Yes!"

A: *"That gets even more disturbing!"*

B: "Yes!"

A: *"But this 'Yes'…"*

B: "Yes?"

A: *"…is more than 'Yes'."*

B: "Yes?"

A: *"But what is this 'Yes'?"*

B: "I suggest you go into it."

A: *"This Yes is what I am!"*

B: "Yes!!!!"

A: *"…and it is perfectly okay for what I have become to collapse into what I am?"*

B: "Yes!"

A: *"But then I am immediately what I am!"*

B: "Yes!"

A: *"I feel so good!"*

B: "Yes."

A: *"But this goodness is already what I am!"*

B: "Yes!"

A: *" You mean that I have been running from pillar to post, from one relationship to another to objectively believe I can get what I am when it is here, already?"*

B: "Yes..."

(ends dialogue)

Welcome to the retreat space! Here we discover that time and thought *can* end and no one can do it. It naturally collapses into that that I Am. And that opens What I Am to What I Am.

The Beloved then is the collapse of what I have become into what 'I Am'. This is Self-realisation. Don't expect a great light or some wonderful experience. It is so simple. *This* is What I Am.

The Absolute is absolute knowledge of What I already am - I Am that I Am.

Always keep your 'I' in your own heart.

The Absolute is the knowledge 'I Am'; impossible to think about. It is Reality itself, the Self realising what It is. It has no distance, no time no space. It really is *now*. It is more than the word intimate. It is intimacy itself, no distance between 'What I Am' and 'What I Am' - Oneness. All images and energies collapse into openness. It is the end of what I have become.

It is not another beginning, it is newness, the deeper streaming and outpouring of 'What I Am' is naturally pouring in.

This Body is an Outpouring of Now

This body is not what it seems to be. It is an outpouring
of Now. Never has it had any past to relate to.
Awareness is enforcing the past on this streaming of a
body, Awareness is enforcing the past on the body. to
see how wonderfully pure and intimate we already are?
Why long for Love when you are already it? But you
must enter it.

Tender Openness

As Awareness see that you are aware of the sensation of
what you may call your body. Now close our eyes, isn't
there a lightness within the black that is beyond any
colouration that might appear as an image? Is it not true,
as Awareness knowingly abiding in the heart there is
tender openness within what appears to be a body?
Is it not instant?

The more Awareness looks within, without any need,
the inner doors open and Awareness becomes more
finely aware of a different kind of body. Forms are not
so defined. Amongst this, as Awareness enters within,
there may be discomfort on some levels.

When you, Awareness, are utterly fine with discomfort,
don't focus on it and have no need for it to disappear,
more opens within.
Then you are, as Awareness, entering not only your
own body but you are entering the larger body of this
apparent group of people-beings. You are opening as
that larger body to the body of humanity. It simply goes

deeper and deeper. We are beginning to know or understand, there is not 'someone doing this'. It is 'I-Awareness', opening to what I deeply authentically am.

As you soften within the heart and soften in what appears to be a body, there are not only shifts in your Knowing and in Awareness, but there can be energetic shifts in the body as sensations. Soften into *What You Are* and the forms of the appearance of *What You Are* begin to shift, change and re-design the human expression. You have no need of this re-design, it is utterly natural, the new simply begins because there is infinite possibility, for 'I Am infinite'.

We may face levels of 'trying' in our body, where we try to open. Endeavour not to pull out of this. Stay open with what is arising, see how the body is not something to reject. Fully embrace it as Awareness knowingly aware. We may have this sense of a larger body, it is just there, this deepening of our Knowing-Aware amongst any discomfort that may come or go. It is so simple.

Day Two

*"Light doesn't penetrate shadow, it permeates it,
in other words, it is the ground for all things to appear.
That is the 'I' that 'I Am', the one listening to these
words now."*

Light Shining as 'I'

There is really only the experience 'I Am', I Am That I
Am. Then it seems to become individuated and seems to
personalise experience, but the light of what one is can
shine up through the self and the person, entirely free of
self-experience. The original light of Awareness shining
as 'I' is moving and it *can* speak. It certainly sees and
knows and it knows no 'other'.

Cemetery Symmetry

The first ground of this retreat is recognising the
'cemetery'. A few first openings are taking place, you
come into Being and instantly: the cemetery.

I know you all would like to arrange your death and
decide that it is going to be like *this* or like *that*. No, it
is going to be like *it is*.

You will see the cemetery differently. You will begin to
see symmetry in the cemetery. It is the opening to the
beyond, which is what you deeply are.

One With and As Being

To be one with Being is not an escape. To be one with
Being is to be one *as* Being. That means you are no
longer projecting 'I have a shadow' or 'someone has a
shadow'. You find the intelligence and compassion to
speak openly and freely of what you know, but this
doesn't mean you are going to be heard. It doesn't mean
you're going to be seen. It doesn't mean there is any
outcome, ever. Life moves; sometimes the weather is
calm, sometimes there is a hurricane.

Magnificence

Awakening is where I come from and where I go to
with each and every breath. When we awaken, we are
given a magnifying glass. For you, maybe I am that.

In a retreat space, everything begins to be magnified so
that you can see and know 'What Is' directly.
Be utterly fascinated with it and within that fascination,
realise what it is made of, which is the one who's
listening to these words now.

Do you know what magnifying means? Magnificence.
There is only the magnificence of 'What Is' and that
One is at the heart and soul of each and every one of us.
You will always discover this in aloneness. Then you
discover you are not alone. You are that One. From that
moment on, everything begins to unfold to realise
'What Is' and it knows no end.

Mudras
The Form Reality Practice

What a mudra is, is what the body is. It is a symmetry of Being, a shape of Being, not the shape of a body.

The movement of The Form is this; it is the shape of Being, not the body but the body takes the form of the shape of Being in its symmetry. You discover in The Form that the flow of the encounter with Reality has within it a divine symmetry that is the display of all life within the universe. Vast systems appear in the universe, vast symmetrical patterns of the expression of divinity. The human body is that, mainly unrealised and unintegrated but *this* is its highest possibility.

Day Three

*"What You Are is totally unfamiliar, utterly unknown.
It is called Now."*

Distraction

Q: *When I am seeing a pattern and I don't want to
engage it or not give power to it and remain in the
Knowing, there is a level of distraction. I know I am
'no-thing' but when I 'want' to stay in the Knowing it
becomes a distraction, which doesn't let me abide in
what you have called 'absence'.*

B: You are saying that the distraction doesn't make you
absent?

Q: Yes I am not remaining in the absence.

B: Absence is all there is. You cannot *remain* in the
absence. It is impossible because absence is all there is!
How can you remain in it? You don't *go there*. You
shed, you unveil, you surrender. You cannot go to
absence. You recognise that it is all there is. There is
actually no one here. It is the end of colouring
experience.

This is a good enquiry. What distraction is, is the belief
that you are 'someone'. What distraction is, is the belief
that there are others that are causing you distraction.
What distraction is, is the belief that there are others
who can stop you from 'having' absence, which is pure
peace. You want others to stop distracting you so that

you can have some peace. You believe that peace is for yourself, but it is not for yourself because your self is also made of absence. Whilst you keep thinking about yourself you will believe that you are *not* absence.

Awareness creates the distraction to maintain the division between the sense of self and the deeper knowing. It believes that it must find what it is in the manner that it *likes*, which creates an opposite of dislike. So it is continually seeking. It seeks absence in things and it is the things that you lose.

What you actually lose is the idea that there are things and that there are others and that things and others fulfil you in the absence of your primary state of openness. Distraction is the belief that love or peace belongs to someone called Raymond. It is Raymond who is the problem, the belief that he actually exists.
Everyone will be hearing this in myriads of different ways in what appears to be personal circumstances. What is actually happening is this: Nothing is meditating all forms back into itself.

It is this: ∞ *(forms the infinity symbol with his hands.)*

All forms are resolved only within Awareness being what it deeply is. Uncontracted open. The contraction will only disappear but essentially *What You Are* has no need for it to disappear in your openness. Within your openness you get to know yourself and the structures you have invented and created to keep yourself separate of being Nothing. You get to experience this, you get to experience those structures.

I am saying that you are not 'someone' who is doing this. This *is* what is happening. It is the return of form to its source and the return of Awareness to realise the first light that is the 'I'.

When we first awaken, an 'undoing' takes place within the cells of our body, within the brain, the nervous system, the heart and within our relationships. We untangle our Awareness from association with objective formed experience. "I like you. I don't like you. I want you. I don't want you. You're good. You're bad.

All that in truth is ever happening is that Nothing is meditating all forms back into itself. Right now, it looks like we are having a conversation but really we are opening to return the forms that are spent. We are returning those forms within our spaciousness and we will *know* ourselves as that happens, as forms return back through the 'I'.

We speak and there is no-one doing it, but in the conversation there is openness; Awareness expands and Knowing becomes its light, which is Love. Now there is a shift of everything into a new place.

Distraction is first off the belief that you are a 'someone' and then all the forms of experience that within your reflective consciousness mirror to you, through polarity or 'like and dislike', that you are a someone. Within this body-mind matrix you are building a dam on the river of the light that *You* essentially *are*.

In awakening everything will come to you, to unblock that flow. No one is doing it! It is Awareness realising what It deeply is.

Most of us won't go this far because it unveils so much and there is seeming great loss in this. It is not the loss of someone. It is the loss of our mind. This is what we are frightened of. But Love is all that is here and Love is functioning for Love is Love and Love clearly is loving.

Q: *What I am really receiving is that the question, which I thought was a personal question, begins to be a question of Consciousness. It feels very detached from the person who can ask a question.*

B: Detached from the person or detached from the belief there is a person? It's all a bit back to front because you have this mind-set that says that you must transform. But there is no one here who can transform!

It is in staying with 'What Is' in utter openness that it all begins to collapse back into your emptiness. What was obscured is revealed. In seeing through the obscuration, the blocks and the dams with no need to get rid of them, you discover what you deeply are.

As these blocks, these structured patterns of 'me', collapse, there is loss. There is the belief that you can lose and you *will* go through that. But it is precisely the collapse of those structures that makes the revealing of this endlessness, this boundlessness absolute. It is the collapse of the belief of 'you' that reveals the light unto itself; I Am that I Am.

An Extraordinary Ordinary Life
The Form Reality Practice

Within The Form, in the moment you 'tune in', this is
not just an encounter with Reality. There is a serenity
within the encounter with Reality for Reality is what
you deeply are. Within that serenity, because it is your
own pure fragrance of Being, Awareness can function
from an entirely deeper dimension and you begin to
have a power of seeing and knowing that is beyond your
usual manner. It is fulfilment.

It is not that you can 'do' anything in this, but I *am*
saying that this re-encodes reality, it seeds this reality
from another height, another depth, another place.

Something utterly deep begins to awaken and it is the
One who is listening to these words. There is this *inner*
opening. As Awareness relates only to this inner
opening of the deeper Knowing, although not
understood, it is able to come from it. This slows down
all the egoic mechanisms within the body-mind and
there is rest. And within that rest an extraordinarily
ordinary life lives. Awareness begins to realise there is
not the seeing of 'things' there is only the knowing of
the Knowing: I Am.

In a very simple real way an entirely different
functionality begins to happen, where there is no one
doing but *it does* very well.

Day Four

*"It is quite difficult to hear that your pain is non-personal. When you are ripe enough you hear it.
It doesn't mean the pain is going to drop away,
it simply means, it is non-personal,
for 'I Am' is not a person.*

The Deep Calling

We have not come to 'seek', there is no seeking here.
We are gathered by 'The Calling', the deep calling. It is
a constant calling. It's in the flowers, it's in the trees,
it's in the hands, it's in the feet, it is everywhere. It is *all*
Reality, seemingly veiled.

The listener, including the speaker *is* Reality, the very
light of Awareness but not 'someone'. It is just an
appearance that I am sitting *here* and you are sitting
there and there are others around. We do know this and
yet the tendency is to forget what we have discovered,
what Awareness realised in its depths of Knowing. It
gets veiled again.

I keep pointing to what is *first* for it is veiled. It *is* here
but it is veiled. What one seeks is what one *is*. The mind
picks this up and believes it is my name, my label, the
'someone' I appear to be, the person, the self and it puts
many constructs around presence. Countless constructs
around What I Am, constantly building the idea 'I am a
someone'.

When we speak together here, we are allowing all these constructs to *just be*, we're not denying them. We are not seeking, not even trying to understand. We are Being together. In that kind of Being-ness together, Awareness becomes sharp, opened. The constructs begin to collapse into what Awareness is; formless and yet formed, because form is made of Awareness, form is veiled Reality.

What's so beautiful about this is that as we are Being together there is a natural unveiling of Awareness to its depth of Knowing. Awareness is opening by not doing anything other than deeply listening, and there is no-one listening, it is just 'listening. Within this listening there is a response at depth, not a depth that is away from 'What Is'. It is just pure depth.

As we begin to truly *be* together, rest together, enquire Reality naturally unveils itself to itself. It may appear to be 'you and I' but really it is what *it* is. It may seem that someone over here or over there has particular experience but the truth is there is *only* the experience of 'What Is', at whatever depth that takes place in.

Am I not 'You'?

Here we are and I appear to be speaking. Am I not *you* speaking? Am I not *you* hearing? Find out how that is. Together, as Being we are unveiling 'What Is'. If you say: "I didn't get what you said.", that is great, it is a door for us to enter together. Then you no longer see 'a teacher'. If there is such a thing as teachers or masters, what they are, is windows to what already is profoundly real, for even a speck of dirt is profoundly real. *All* is veiled or hidden Reality.

Masters are beautiful Beings revealed. Is there anything more to say than that? They are open doors. Windows and doors that no longer have any hinges of identification. They are wide open. That is why in openness, extraordinariness comes out of your mouth, out of your body.

If the surface is made open, in other words non-identification with 'What Is', it's natural for the Being to surface as it were. You speak and know from Being. You might call those people masters but there is no-one there mastering the mind or the condition. There's only 'This that is being what It is', unveiled.

Your Pain is Non-Personal

There is nothing you could ever experience, even great pain, that is not veiled Reality. The mind will tell you otherwise and will constantly construct a person that is a victim of someone else, a victim of circumstances. It is quite difficult to hear that your pain is non-personal. Nonetheless, when we are ripe enough we hear it. It doesn't mean the pain is going to drop away. It simply means it is non-personal for 'I Am *not* a person'. The person is a Reality-movement that has form. In a very real manner there *is* an expression of the totality. Then the person is no longer 'someone' but an apparent individuated wholeness.

Vagueness

Vagueness is veiling 'vacancy'. Self is emptying, which means constructs are collapsing naturally, through Awareness no longer seeking but being present, still and open in this moment called *now*. Nowhere else to go to, nothing to seek. Seeking has ceased.

In that moment one might experience 'vagueness' because there is vacancy and the mind wonders: "What is this nothing?" but it is the one that is listening to these words now. Then the mind will speak and act as vagueness and you might say: "Well nothing is going on for me here. It's all a little bit dull and vague."

Somehow we are very uncomfortable with being totally vacant, which is openness, which is That in which everything appears in and returns to. All is made of vacancy and it is all but vague. Within it is utter passion, not passion for any 'thing' but passion for 'What Is'.

Vagueness is Awareness veiling its entrance to the deep because it has preference on the surface. It wants to keep this idea 'I am a someone'. It is a very good game.

Somehow, in the mystery of it all Awareness is able to know Knowing revealed as deeper reality. It is not a 'thing' but a shining of Reality and in the same moment a level of self-form that is veiled. There is a connection of the deeper Knowing as Awareness with formed experience, a connection with the deeper mystery opening and a level of veiled mystery in terms of the personalisation of experience.

Ripeness

Our meeting is actually a mirror of daily life. There is a
calling here and that calling is constant, whether you are
making a cup of tea or walking at the beach or you are
at work. It is always there. Just pause and you will
know the calling and the opening or you will know
veiled Reality.

There has to be ripeness in all this and paradoxically
there is no-one who is ripe. There is just ripeness. I call
it 'The Calling'.

Being Aware Together

As we simply enter Being-Aware together, Knowing is
no longer tied up as 'knowing someone', knowing a
person, knowing like or dislike, knowing anything.

Knowing begins to deepen and expand in a very
unusual manner as Awareness appearing to be
'someone'. This is because there is the unveiling of
Awareness to the light of its Knowing and in that this
depth of Knowing matches how life is moving on the
surface.

Awareness Constructs Identity

Awareness in the mind constructs an identity through
having experience through time and space. Awareness
puts it all together and it moves as a self-image. It is

electro-magnetic and it is powerful because the listener is Reality itself. Anything it believes in becomes real.

A Living Understanding of 'What Is'

At some point there comes a level of living understanding of 'What Is'. You begin to truly rest. You realise: "My God I'm not the person. The person is a vessel made of what 'I Am', and what I Am speaks and conveys what I am unveiling on the surface and what I am realising in the deep. They are the same one."

It is a veiled reality up on the surface, unveiling itself to itself and there is no-one doing it. Can you see this is the end of suffering and an opening to the wonder and beauty of what truly is?

This forms a new reality within what appears to be humankind, for as one unveils oneself to oneself, the self-level begins to match the Being and Being pours into the self. Now it is made of Being and is no longer a power unto itself. Passion moves, wonder moves, mystery moves, gorgeousness, all pouring from the one Goodness.

About Karma

*Q: What do you see around karma? I was in a yoga
tradition for many years and they say that all that we
have done is coming back to us, the good things and the
bad things...Many masters speak about this.*

B: The idea that you can create karma for someone who
is not actually here is an illusion. You can believe that
you are here and there will be lots of karma. I don't use
the word 'karma', I say, "Keep calm, the game is over".
I say quite simply that the belief that thoughts and
feelings are 'you' is a construct in the mind.

When did who you believe you are appear? If you have
a look at this, you may see that mostly you cannot
remember when you were a child. There will be some
memories but there are huge gaps. That is because you
are Being, not a construct. As a small child there was no
form, you didn't have constructs and there was no
sophistication of mind. You were taught that.

You can't remember when you were a child because you
weren't 'anyone'. You were the enjoyment of Being;
completely innocent. With the growing sophistication of
the brain you enter conditionality, which you must but
you never *actually* enter the condition. It just moves
because of *What You Are*, which is entirely beyond it.

Awareness arises, forms arise in Awareness; it seems
that someone is arising, it seems that someone takes
form. As Awareness you begin to believe that the
movement of this level is 'you'. You begin to really
believe it and take it on, whatever the culture, the

religion, or the circumstance. You do this until at some
point you yearn to break free of it all but you *are* free of
it all.

Simply Not You

Karma is believing you need something else other than
'What Is'. You mentally build objects of experience and
you imprint the need to feel in a certain way of polarity.
You are constructing karma; negative and positive
forces when really you are already 'Pure-I' and beyond.

You don't have to get rid of this construction, or karma
as you called it, because it is simply 'not you'. When
You-Awareness sees through all this and responds to
Being you are no longer building a separate sense, a
programmed, patterned self that keeps informing you.

Karma is the idea that you are 'someone' and you are
building objective experiences around positive and
negative vibes and vibrations, which you are
constructing. You Awareness, not 'someone'. Very
naturally, a sense of self is constructed out of the belief
in polarity or need or want. As a baby-being that didn't
happen. The so-called building of the body happened
naturally. It is an utter mystery. It builds around this
impulse of Awareness moving to this level of its own
light.

You don't see a baby moving, you see aware Being
moving. And when you see a baby sleep deep, you are
not seeing a baby sleep deep, you are seeing depth of
Being. It seems to form as the baby or 'you and I', but it

is how this level naturally forms what Awareness *is* in the light of Being. It is conditional up on this level, in other words it passes, it comes and goes.

In truth, there is no-one here undoing those constructions or karmic levels. They just naturally fall away because they cannot be sustained. Are you still going to be around a hundred years from now? Can you just stay in this body? Do you need to sustain this body or will it naturally collapse? Collapse into what? It is just a movement of formed presence being aware, an appearance. You feel the patterned idea of this level, this society that you have constructed by belonging to it. It is held together by Awareness. If you didn't hold anything together in terms of experience, Pure Awareness would simply be unveiled and realised and you will always discover that it is *You*.

Real Medicine

Q: *I am thinking about all the things that are happening in the world. People are hurting and killing each other and destroying the planet and when you say karma doesn't exist then it means for me that everybody can just go ahead with it all.*

B: Would you like to hear that YOU are killing the people, you are killing the planet?

Q: *No, actually.*

B: Well you are. Because you *are* everyone. You see everybody believes that they are a 'someone' involved in all this. You are not 'someone'. You can play this game, but I guarantee that your body will drop away and you will realise so much more.

The planet doesn't need to be saved, what needs to be saved is you from believing you are 'someone'. Although even that is not quite true, for in truth there is no one here. You are doing this in your mind and your mind is appearing as your personalising of experience. And then yes, it *does* show up on this surface. It shows up as seeming destruction, but you cannot destroy what is real.

When you begin to get this, in the ease of you dropping it all, Being fills what appears to be form and you begin to truly see 'What Is'. You see through all of it. Then it is not 'someone' who will change this, as if it needs to change, it will naturally change because of where *you* now come from. If you believe there are others doing this, there will be more negativity because there are no others. *You* are doing this. You see how difficult this is to hear? You are doing it by believing you are separate from your partner, or from the chair, from anyone or anything. All this has to be seen through.

You are every human being on the planet, you are humanity, on this level and deeper. Respond to what you *first* are and you will see what you first are outshine what your mind tells you is happening. Be interested in that, because your mind wants you to focus on changing others and not on seeing you and knowing yourself. It gives you a right to be unhappy and someone else is bound to be the cause of it. It is not the truth.

I have a sign here, its rather like what is written on packets of cigarettes these days: 'Smoking is bad for your health'. This sign says: "Realising will deconstruct your sense of self" and you will be *knowing* yourself.

No one is to blame. Blame is a very deeply engrained idea on this level and yet through all this Awareness is unveiling its light to itself. It just looks like it is not. The war you are having 'in there' and the war you might have with a partner, in your family, at work is the same war as the wars you see in the world. It just seems to be on a bigger scale. It is the same thing, the same movement. It is difficult to hear this.

The pain that one may have is not 'someone's' pain. There is no personal pain. It is how this level is actually the movement of the beyond unveiling itself. It seems to be a personal body, a personal nervous system, a personal mind and a personal attitude. That is veiled Reality. Not easy to listen to. One must enter it all consciously aware. You must. Nothing is happening to you. You must enter it, otherwise you are still seeking, veiling.

What you are looking for is *What You Are* and it is in everything. The moment you stop, there is the opening to 'What Is'. That is the return of what you called karma or patterning. It is returning to no one. You are now available because of the ripeness and the opening to being no one. Then patterns return to the 'I' they come from. They return. The deeper you go, the more unveiling there is, the more patterns deconstruct within your awareness of Being and your experience of a sense of self. The mind is telling you something is happening

to you. Real medicine is not discovering ways for
people to be comfortable but for the people to realise
what they *are*. That is real medicine. The flowers are
real medicine, the sky, the ocean, air, sound, the birds,
music… Real medicine is being in presence where
everything is alive and unveiled.

The Person

The person is the outer mouthpiece, the vocal cord of
what is happening in the self, what is opening in the
heart, what is deeper than all of this; Reality. All this is
made of it, it is not hidden, it is all within this and it
comes and it speaks and it appears to be 'someone' and
it is having a conversation with itself right now.

Day Five

"We are not just people, we are transformative vehicles of the universal human. This is a universal human and the evolution of what appears to be human is also the evolution of what appears to be the universe."

Observation and Softness

In seeing, in knowing, in observing, there is unveiling. Simple, unveiling. Forms unveil Reality, for forms are made of Reality, the light of Awareness.

They unveil, they flower. Our attention mostly stays with a believed observer as somebody, looking at a form that seems to be solid. Our movement on the surface then begins to be wrapped around the identification with a seeming person having a seeming self and a seemingly solid form. Then we look at someone as if they are someone. We look at a thing as if it is a thing. Our attention stays on the surface.

Sit quietly and soften and see, soften and observe, soften and know. It all points to the same '*no-thing-ness-thing*'; Awareness knowing aware. See how mind in a flash, creates Awareness as a 'somebody', and Knowing as a 'thing'. A thing of a somebody, a me, and an object. That flash is taking place within spacious Awareness, that knows and sees and is not observing. It just *Is*. Knowing, seeing, aware. The mechanism of the body-mind puts it all together as a construct, of 'someone' knowing and seeing.

Here is a simple soft observation then: I sit at the back of the room this morning. I just sit. Not doing anything. Things are happening, there is seeing and knowing. Then people come into the room.

This is my observation as they come in. They begin to see each other, and meet and as they see each other and meet, they begin to greet, speak and 'do'. And within that they begin to talk, and a lot of energy is spent. They must spend it, it has to be spent and as they spend the energy, the field of apparent noise, gets louder and louder, and the energy of what is being spent builds. It just gets spent and spent and then it comes to a crescendo and then all the noise and chatter simply collapses.

The energy is spent and collapses into this indescribable spacious nothing. The believed bodies soften and soften, no longer are the bodies a drone of a person but a lovely expression of unspeakable wonder and beauty. The bodies, rather than being a drone of a society, a culture, a religion, a somebody, a family or of humans, they are now this melting tender gentleness that every drone actually longs for. Now there is a wonderful display of the artfulness of Love, as the bodies just turn into this softness of Life-Aware. It is quite a dance.

Mostly our attention just sits on the surface. We are dying to collapse and we *will* collapse when we die. But then we find we don't die as Awareness, but the forms of our obsession do. But don't they collapse when one goes into deep dreamless sleep? Don't they collapse, when our attention as Awareness is into where all this comes from, rather than just on the surface, supporting

the mirage, the obsession, the neurosis that we are all
separate, and we are all 'someones'?

All the energy gets spent, and is spent in many, many
ways. Maybe in war, maybe in illness, maybe in cancer.
It is all the struggle of knowing there is more than just
this neurosis of believing I am someone on the surface,
this drone of appearance.

This morning's observation was wonderful. You can
just be still, and you see how everything is taking place,
and where it all returns to. Regardless of what takes
place, all this returns to where it all comes from.

With a little observation, a little Knowing, you will see
that your attention Awareness, is simply held in the
surface belief that you are someone. It is held there and
you are just sharing, the *linear* rather than the *vertical*.
You are sharing thousands of years of experience of a
self, of self-experience. Behind it all, at all times, is the
one who is listening to these words now and all that
spent energy of the belief 'I am a particular someone',
continually collapses, in the apparent death of the
apparent someone.

The Deepest Flowering

Gently look at the ocean. Waves look to be all on their
own. This is a different wave from that wave and that
other wave over there. You think that is a wave but
that's really a movement of energy. Do you think that is
a wave? Go a little bit deeper. It's a movement of
energy. Then go into the energy. Now you see the

energy moving as a wave. Go deeper, and there is the wave moved by energy. Go deeper. Is there anything moving here? Go ever deeper into the ocean. It is so still. Did you ever wake up in the morning like that? Have you seen that in the birth of a baby? Have you seen how a baby settles back into the deep as it hasn't identified with the wave yet?

We identify with all this movement but we are not aware that we are doing this. We identify with the movement called 'my feet are moving' or 'my hands are moving', or 'my head's moving'. We don't see through it. We have not really opened, observed and actually seen that this body-mind-manifestation is a flower and it lives in a garden. The garden is in no-thing whatsoever and yet it is expressed and then it returns.

On the surface there are patterns of identification and we believe all those thoughts and feelings are what we are. But they are the leftovers!

Maybe even war is the leftover of the thoughts and feelings that everybody thinks are other people's thoughts and feelings or the ones we insist are *my* thoughts and *my* feelings. Maybe this is what war is, the struggle with ourselves and not the openness to what we *are*, amongst the struggle.

In openness, patterns simply collapse, just like a wave, because they are no longer identified with. There is simply no energy so it all collapses back into the deep.

Enter!

I invite you to know your hand. What is the finger
without the use of the mind? What is the palm? What is
the arm, what is the leg? What is the face?
Enter fully, even though there may be resistance, which
is always of the self or the mind and not of what you
first deeply are. Enter! As Awareness enters, the body
becomes spacious and open. There is more joy and
sincerity.

Then when you wave at someone, it is not just a shallow
wave, it is an entrance into the deep where the meeting
truly is. That fills up the body, fills up the relating, fills
up the heart, fills up the room, fills up this humanness.
It is the shining of what one is, what you have always
longed for. It has never ever been separate.

A Mudra of The Present

Isn't the body, even its shape, a code of the deep, a
flowering of the deep?

Rather than *look* at movement, *know* it. When this hand
is not identified with, it is so much more than
somebody's hand. It doesn't have any shape. Even the
sensation of a shape collapses. There is just this
spacious openness. If you move that hand now, you
will see that mind says "my hand is moving". It is
making the hand a position, belonging to someone that
that hand is on. Yes?

Awareness tends to keeps its attention in thought, feeling and sensation in time and space, as if time and space circles around its body-mind identity. In this we become rather like a robot, running from one time to another, running from one experience to the next, trying to get what we believe we need to be *what we are.*

When that attention drops into what appears to be *within*, there is a softening, a warming, an opening, a dissolving. Instead of attention having a centre, attention falls away and there is opened Knowing-Aware. Up on the surface this is translated as one's body, one's hand, one's feet, one's head, one's eyes, one's nose, one's life, one's friends, the ocean. It is short of nothing and full of wonder!

Your nervous system is a pathway, your mind is a pathway, your blood vessels are pathways, your toes are pathways, your fingers are pathways, your eyes are pathways. Everything is a pathway in this body!

You will see that all those pathways are full of old ways. One is not living what one is, but living some idea of a collective life over thousands of years, a collection of ideas of what one should do, how one should think, how one should operate, how one should function. It is a neurosis. *This* is actually our struggle and our pain. The pain in the body, mind, the 'pain in the neck' and in our relating is that we are constantly giving our attention to old pathways. It is like a groove in the subtleties of what is a body.

When you just put our attention somewhere else, other than just the surface, to the heart for instance, or into

what the form of the fingers are, the form of what the
toe is or what the chest is, you enter more than a form.
You enter what form is made of and what it is the outer
expression of, which is of the one who is listening to
these words now.

Veils fall away, old paths collapse, and new openings,
new pathways open in the body. Now the bodies seem
to be the shape of a deepening, encoded entirely
differently. A mudra of the present, where what is
coursing through it and pouring from it is a way of
Being. It is full of delight and it has no objective
experience.

Day Six

"What is presence is the truth that
What I Am is nowhere else but here."

Divinely Inspired

Who is there in truth, who can say: "That was my
mother's stuff, that was my father's stuff, that was my
ancestry?"

Yes, there can be a recognition that patterns are passed
down from father to son, from mother to daughter, from
one nation to another but it is far deeper than that. Go a
little deeper and a new place, a place-less place opens.
Bring your attention there.

When the mind tells you that you are looking at
someone you know, it brings up the past to make that
person *known*, but that is either *You* knowing *You*, or
your need to know another in the past. This is the
constant battle.

Become bigger than that, go deeper than that! Self then
becomes the possibility of Awareness awakening to
what *it* deeply *is*. It is seen to be a no-self-Self. Nobody
is actually there as a collection of ideas, patterned by
personalisation of experience, as a somebody, as a
family, as a religion, as a nation or even as a human.

Then we *are* truly human, not *a human* but humanity
divinely inspired. Divinely inspired means Awareness is
knowing more than the tension held in surface beliefs.

Attention is dropped below the known into the simple aware Knowing knowing Knowing. Inspiration pours from the unknown. Inspiration is the outpouring of Being that never becomes anything or anyone. All this is simply an appearance that manifests that that is beyond appearance. This is the wonder of this life.

This is where you really know you love. There is no need to search for it, no need to get it. You begin to see and recognise the old pathways of the neurosis of believing 'I am a particular human'. Then you see the wonder of this, you will laugh more, you will cry more, you will wonder more, you will undo more, and it is *all* great. Greatly terrible, greatly wonderful. There is greatness in each and every one of us, *right here* expressing what *it* is.

Day Seven

*"'What You Are' cannot fail to turn up on your
blackboard, in your classroom, in your life".*

From Power to Pure Being Aware

When we were very young, we had a fascination with
things, not because they were 'things' but there was a
profound quality of joy in the knowing of Knowing.
Your joy as a child wasn't coming from naming things,
wasn't coming from you having a name. It was the pure
joy of Being. As a very young child you had no
objective sense of self. Everything was streamed by
Being, pure innocence.

When you were a child, you also had a different kind of
listening. There was simply a fascination with life in
innocence. Objects of experience did not have power
because there was nothing arising that was not of the
quality of your Beingness.

There might be touches of this Knowing within your
own body now, because it points to what embodiment
truly is. Your body is a body of Being, a body of
Awareness and through the genius instrument of the
brain, Consciousness turns Being into sense perception.

In innocence, objects had no power. They were the
streaming of Being. You loved this life of being a child,
the sensing child of the universe.

There was a little power in the emotion. You can see that in a very young child, but that is the power of the instrument. There was no object that had power. Thoughts and feelings did not have power, your toys or your teddy bear did not have power. It was all the streaming of Being manifest. Everything was arising in Being, moved in Being. That is the Love you see and enjoy in a child.

The moment you were introduced into *having* power, you began to know the power of polarity, of like and dislike. You were knowing it in innocence and you saw its practice. You saw the practice of empowerment through duality. You saw it in the world, you saw it in what appeared to be your mother and father but you did not recognise it.

You were gradually weaned off of being innocent and taught the use of power. There is nothing wrong in this, we are just looking at *how* this is. You began to extract power from objects. Whereas before it was in Being, now it was 'my' teddy bear. That is power.

You began to believe that the power, the energy of *What You Are* is in objects. All objects are actually animated by the power of Being present, but the moment that that power is taken for a sense of self, there is no Beingness in it. The power shifts, the Awareness shifts from the power of being innocence, where there is no object, to having power for a sense of self.

Beingness is innocent. It does not *do*; it just is Pure Being. Pure Being animates the cosmos and yet it is beyond it. It pours in and animates it.

Without knowing this, you extracted power from an object and you, Awareness, gave the power of that object, which once belonged to Being, to a sense of self. That is the first moment you truly knew power. You began to be in objective power and you built a self-centre out of objective power.

Within *The Form Reality Practice* you experience power and tremendous energy. That is the power of your being. The energy of the body is really the energy of the universe and how it manifests.

In the practice of *The Form*, the energy of the power no longer belongs to a self that is observing the universe but actually becomes the power of the universe, the universe and its Beingness. It is a trinity. That power is not *used*. There is no one there to use it.

This is empowerment returned to Being. The sweetness of Being begins to flood Awareness and Awareness is fulfilled by the fragrance of its Being. Power is no longer used in duality. In the movement of *The Form* and indeed in daily life, when Awareness is awake to 'What Is' and the movement of life *as it is*, it discovers where power comes from and returns to. You as Awareness, discover how power follows you where you give yourself to.

You have to see that power can also be veiled. It is veiled until it is unleashed on you. If you have a sore point in the body, that is power leaking. It begins to unveil not only Being-Aware, but also power following where Awareness is giving its sense of self to.

We are taught this but not in an awake manner. We are taught to have power and then taught to give power to a particular society, a particular relationship, a particular culture, a particular candidate. We are taught to give our power away with the idea that that power will be returned to us, but it is all given to a sense of self. I call that sense of self 'the world' and it is not the earth. This is very subtle but it begins to grow in our knowing of 'What Is'.

To be *all in* in the practice of The Form is to be *all in* the moment, *all in* the life, *all in* 'What Is'. When you are *all in*, you begin to discover where power goes, where it flows, what it is given to. In giving to Being, sweetness flows and Awareness knows its own fulfilment. Being one with Being-Aware is the fulfilment everyone seeks but we tend to seek this as and for the separate sense of self.

Within the practice, we say: "Go to where this goes to." We are not talking about the person, but about a relationship of Awareness to Being and Knowing and not to a separate sense of self. Power given to Being is powerful in that it returns Awareness to what It deeply is. It is the only fulfilment there is.

You must be *all in* it. Every movement is power returned to Pure Being-Aware. The power that makes all this possible is the same power that expresses the universe, moves the universe, is the life of the universe and evolution of all the beings within it. It is the power of Love.

Day Eight

*"The entrance of the unknown
is only in the death of the known.
And in the death of the known the
human is transfigured and remade in Being."*

Fear of The Unseen

Why do we fear or ignore the unseen? Is it because
there is more of the unseen than of the known and it is
vast without beginning and end? Is this our fear?

It has not become obvious to us, when we are so
practiced in being somebody, that the unseen is
naturally arising in the Awareness that knows it is
aware and aware of the forms of Reality.

It is not obvious to us because we are so sensitised to
sense-perception alone. What I am pointing to most
wouldn't even call sense-perception but fact or reality.
Take a good look, is sense perception deception? Is
sense perception deception or is it only deception if we
are not perceptive to what we deeply are?

Well then, is it okay to drop or let go of everything?
Well, surely it is because we drop it every night we go
to sleep, do we not? Don't we drop everything?
Everything is left behind. Not one single object survives
deep dreamless sleep, not a single one.

"How did you sleep? "

"Oh, I have no memory of that but I know I slept deeply."

"What do you mean by that?"

"There were no dreams, no images and no movement. I know I wasn't there as 'someone', but I am aware of the deep."

If you truly looked into deep dreamless sleep, would that destabilise your dreamed life? Does the truth that everything disappears destabilise your dreamed life or do new forms of Reality arise as Awareness becomes aware of form?

Is it fully clear to you that in deep dreamless sleep there is no dreamer? In deep dreamless sleep everything disappears, the dreamed person, the dreamed culture, the dreamed religion, the dreamed partner, the dreamed everything. Yet we love it.

What is this love of that dream-less place-less place? It is the love of the truth that it is what one Is, already whole, already One.

When this is utterly clear, there is an immense enjoyment, the pure enjoyment of 'not having a self'. In truth, *not having a self* is our greatest joy. Then what self-concern can one have?

You Are Nothing-Aware

The moment Awareness or Nothing-Aware becomes aware of form, the forms shape-shift all the way from the metaphysical and the biological up into this actuality. It brings finer lights of deeper reality up to this level that is currently labelled 'human'. Everything is shifted and changed by Awareness realising form. Awareness brings with it the unseen that has an entirely different Beingness.

The moment of coming out of or going into to sleep is our best shot at being fully aware of 'forming' and aware of 'forming dissolving'. It is a place or instance in which Awareness can discover the 'tipping out' and the 'tipping into' form. As you drop into sleep, forms dissolve into Awareness tipping in or spilling back into the unseen realms of its own Being. In waking up Awareness tips into the forming, which actually only arises within its own Awareness.

As you are, here and now, is it not true you are Nothing-Aware and this is the awake state? *What You Are* is Nothing-Aware. It is very much the same as any instant morning or night, it is here now. Morning and night in truth are an invention of the mind that believes in light and dark, seen and unseen. Nothing-Aware is the total availability of what is right now.

It *is* possible, but only as Nothing-Aware, for deeper levels of the unseen Reality to move 'up to this level' in response to Nothing-Aware aware of forming. But it must remain Awareness only and never become someone.

That is Love knowing, moving, manifesting the deep and it is the *Now*.

The Abundance We Seek

Our pain and suffering as humans is simply because we believe we are someone. Yet Nothing-Aware is the abundance we seek and fail to find as humans because we have to *discover* that we are Nothing-Aware and all forms arise in Nothing-Aware.

Phenomenal forms arise and resolve in the Beingness of Nothing-Aware. Ongoing transformation is integral within Nothing-Aware and takes place through non-identification with the forms of experience.

The Shape of Another Place

What configures this life? How does this life takes shape? How does this body take shape?

Is this body within itself or is its shape of another place? Is this body not the shape a code of a deeper reality, not just the surface reality? Deeply look and see...

Is the body not the bringer of the body-less? Are the eyes not the seeing of the unseen? Is the breath not the breathing of emptiness?

On Death

What death does, especially if it is very close and intimate, death opens the Awareness to finer realms of Being.

A finer realm of Being is also the, let's call it hard disc of the download of your ancestry, the package of patterning that we all believe is 'us'. Often this opens when someone you have loved passes and definitely when your mother or father pass on. The ancestry that Being-Aware did not transform within the movement of life in a body, is passed on to humanity. It is passed on through what appears to be someone's child.

You see, the movement of the body is not just 'someone' moving. The body is a transformative vehicle of Pure Consciousness. The body-mind cannot *do* any of this, it all occurs through Awareness.

Awareness downloads deeper levels of unseen Reality in coming up to form. It is the pure intelligence that is evolving in the human level and it must do, otherwise this could not form. The experience of 'being someone' is essential to stabilise the Beingness of 'being no-one'. It is paradoxical but this is what happens, because this body-mind system needs the deeper support of experience, at first.

Awareness itself then downloads up into the metaphysical and the biological, up into the formed level, *where* it is now coming from. Awareness is multidimensional, omnipresent.

Through the shock of someone passing, in a being such
as yourself and in the subtlety of what you are speaking
of, you become aware of openings; points of entry and
exit of deeper domains of Being. We are not just people,
we are transformative vehicles of the universal human.
This is a universal human and the evolution of what
appears to be human is also the evolution of what
appears to be the universe.

When we think we are human we are using the mind of
humanness that is an evolving vehicle through
experience, but through Awareness awakening beyond
the human, a profounder light of intelligence begins to
inform this vehicle of what truly is.

The human then is transcended but included and the
finer realms of Being fill up the human on every level.
A human becomes divinely inspired.

You are all divinely inspired. Any 'holding' is 'not
dying to the known'. You won't let your objective sense
pass on. It means you are not truly clear that the
entrance of the unknown is only in the death of the
known. And in the death of the known the human is
transfigured and remade in Being.

A simple movement such as picking up a glass then is
not just a movement, the seeing of another is not just the
seeing of another, the whole movement of the body,
from the toes to the nose, from mind to emotion, from
energy to Consciousness, Awareness, from blood to
bone, it is all a transformative vehicle of transcendence.

Ancestry then drops into what appears to be 'someone', but it is a Beingness-Aware and the movement of life is transforming the codes of reality from this reality and uploading a deeper realm of Being. That is the new life! All these doors begin to open and have life. You are not seeing the tremendous speed in which a door opens, you transcend this reality and then immediately include it.

You believe you go to sleep, but you do not, you simply go into a deeper place of Awareness. It is quite natural for the passing of an apparent father or mother or friend to open such profundity in you but it could be through anyone, for there are thousands of people dying right now! Can't you feel the download, the entry and the exit? So many doors are wide open and we are blind to them.

Day Nine

*"Can we meet all of life, meet this 'What Is'
with no inner boundary?
Is that possible?
I say it is."*

Boundless Real Life

When you meet 'What Is' as Awareness true to the Knowing within the heart, boundaries just drop away. Not through a 'doing' but through recognition and openness.

Boundaries drop away, even the boundary of the body, is no longer a boundary. You-Awareness, are passing through all the ports that are opened within you, for everywhere there are portholes into profound boundlessness.

You discover that the capacity to share this life is boundless. You are now available for *real* life because as Awareness you are no longer distracted by the need of a personal boundary inside and outside.

On the outside that personal boundary aligned with openness within is perfectly fine. An awakened life begins to pour. There is a returning *in* and in Awareness returning in, there is a pouring *out* of that return.

Things change on every level of the self and the person. There is integration, there is a meeting in Being and the Being is the forming and there is 'no-one' here.

What is a Hand?

What is a hand? I am asking Awareness, it is not
'someone' asking 'someone'. It is an open question
direct and immediate. Close our eyes and come to the
knowing of 'hand'.

See if you can find a hand. Awareness, can you find a
hand? Awareness, open your eyes. Mind says that is 'a
hand'. Close your eyes. What is it now? Is it an 'it'?
What is your aware experience of 'that'? You might
still have a mental idea of 'hand' but with your eyes
closed, is this a hand or is this a flow of a band of multidimensional reality?

Now open your eyes and look at your hand, move it
very, very slowly. When the hand moves slowly,
doesn't Awareness disengage mind to know what
'hand' is? Have you ever seen a baby do this? I could sit
for hours watching a little baby look at its hand because
it doesn't name it. It sees an object, but there is no
subject knowing an object called 'hand'. There is just
the knowing of this level of reality, 'figured' in that it
has form but within the awake innocence in children,
there is a figure of a form of that that has not been
figured out. This is pure Seeing and pure Knowing.

You are knowing what the mind says is 'hand' but you
are knowing more than the form of the hand. Your
attention can be of this level of Awareness as *forming*
and it can be of the unseen. Is it the unseen seeing this
right now?

Go back to the innocence of a child looking at the hand and you are able to be fully in Awareness, in unseen Reality. Is this then somebody's hand, or is it the movement of the deep, formed? It is forming *now*, it doesn't have time or space in it. This is the uniqueness or the wonder of the brain that forms the Now in instant forms of Now. Real form, it does not pass away because it only is *now*.

When Awareness Sees the Knower of Reaction

Awareness has the ability to contain thoughts and feelings as an identity. Awareness can contain Reality in the sense of a person, in its endeavour to keep the sensation of personalising *the same*.

Up on this apparent human level then, the natural joy of Being is not known, not felt. The boundary on the surface is condensed experience, believed to support the belief: "I am 'someone'. I am held together by a boundary within and I must not let boundlessness or the unknown in. I must stay known. I must stay familiar."

It is all the mind. Awareness can see or register a reaction in the holding together of 'being someone', being a self, a person, through accumulated experience of like and dislike. There is the endeavour to keep all these likes and dislikes confined within this boundary. It is actually like being stifled to death. Limited. And somewhere all this is being registered as 'me'. So when we begin to open and awaken we may meet resistance. Resistance is always of the self and person. Resistance known by Awareness is perfectly okay. It is knowledge.

Is it: "I have resistance"' or is it: "There is resistance."?
Awareness lights up in its true awakening. "Oh look,
there is resistance!"

Now Awareness can see that the resistance is in the
sense of self, person. When Awareness sees that there is
reaction, Awareness will begin to see that there is a
knowing of reaction, and this knowing is free of
reaction. Immediately then, instead of identifying with
the reaction, it begins to turn towards the knowing of
reaction. "How do I know there is reaction?"

As Awareness turns to see the Knower of reaction, there
is no self to know any reaction. In Awareness turned in
the direction of *'who is it that knows'*, there is a natural
pull towards the knowing of Knowing. Instead of
focusing on reaction in a sense of self, it turns towards
the light of Knowing. I call this 'The Calling'. As it
turns to the Knowing, all there is, is the light of
knowing Knowing-Aware, utterly free of self.

Awareness then quite naturally drops away the focus on
the sense of self. It doesn't focus on the Knowing, it is
consumed by Knowing, pulled by Knowing, called by
Knowing for Knowing knows no one, knows no self,
knows no person and knows no thing. It knows it
knows. Pure light of Awareness knowing Knowing;
radiant fullness.

Awareness begins to see that all reactions are only in
the self and person. It begins to discern Knowing and
discovers that Knowing only knows the brightness of
knowing Knowing-Aware. Awareness begins to move
into knowing the Knowing-Aware. It fills out the

Knowing and the Knowing fills out the Awareness and *that* is actually 'What Is'.

Day Ten

"The Heart is not a place but a door to Pure Openness."

A Finite Movement of Infinity

This surface level is a wave on the sea that doesn't change. There is this finite movement, which is an arising of an infinite sea. Somehow, without doing anything Awareness, you and I, is able to know this moment of humanness and there is relatedness to what humanness is a wave of.

In that moment we are seeing this finite moment that seems to pass away from that that does not pass away. Infinite in nature, unmoved by the movement of a wave. If this is becoming clear to you, the wave is moved by the unmovable, the infinite sea of Consciousness-Aware.

The wave belongs to the infinite although this wave called 'I' or 'me' or 'we' passes. It is infinite in nature but finite in form. There comes a point when we become disinterested in this finite wave we once called 'me'. We may still come back into it here and there, but within a field of experience awakening to the ocean from which it arises. All experience now belongs to the deeper nature of the Consciousness aware in this moment. Then our awareness is rooted in the deep and the deep is seen to move the wave called the cosmos, the universe, the earth, humanity or 'I' in humanness.

No Need to Understand

What begins to take place is that there is no need to
know how I know. There is no need to understand
Knowing. What is form? Why do we do this and why
do we do that and how can we do this and how can we
do that? When there is no need to know, Knowing
opens.

Knowing opens in one's awareness because it *is* the
light of Awareness. Now there is real living openness,
any form is seen as the light of the Self. This is actually
Self-realisation. There is no seer, no knower, just 'That'.
The veil has disappeared.

Then the apparent return to the perception of humanness
is full of the realising of Being. It has happened to no-
one but now a cell within the forming of humanness is
moved somewhat differently and Awareness has access
to more than the familiar. A very unusual Living
Awareness.

Day Eleven

*"All that you see has power of You in it
but not 'you as a someone'. Everything is a movement
of light and energy manifesting the One.
Cells of the One are awakening to what it is and
returning."*

A Singular Movement

Attention given to a thought or a feeling, energises that
thought and feeling and rebuilds it in a structure that
gives it reality. Awareness giving attention makes it real
for Awareness is the light of Reality. Light expresses
what Awareness can come aware into, this vast
knowing Nothing. Nothing-Aware.

When Awareness identifies with a thought or a feeling,
an image of a 'someone' with the image of events that
seemed to have happened to this 'someone', the image
seems to have reality. Tremendous power is given to
that image. This is how even the universe is held
together as an image, as an objective reality. It looks
like it is 'out there' but the universe can never be
defined by what the mind interprets it to be.

In the same way an image or a pattern of fear is
enforced by the attention of Awareness within an idea
or past event. Being aware as a somebody makes that
time, that space, that event real, energised. In truth, *all*
energy is forming this moment of 'I Am', creating real
form of Awareness rested within its own light.
Existence is seen to be whole, one with Knowing-

Aware; not dual. A singular movement that arises out of
Awareness, made of the light of the Self; Pure Being
Knowing.

Someone

The 'someone' is built out of past images. Not just in
this single stream of the life you seem to have since you
were apparently born and that will apparently die, but
this entire conditional realm of Reality.

It is a finite wave, an appearance in an infinite ocean.
Our attention can drop as a wave while the wave has
movement of forming. Then Awareness is knowing the
wave not from knowledge of existence in terms of
linear time and experience but all attention is given to
Pure Knowing, the immediacy of Being one with
Knowing. Awareness one with Knowing is whole. It is
not passing away.

The wave passing is the forming of Reality up on this
level of existence. The forms change but the energy,
power and Consciousness that the forms are made of is
constant. Find out what that constant is. Is it 'not 'I'
who am listening to these words now? Does that 'I' not
point even beyond being 'I'?

There is a calling in this, the calling of Truth. The
calling is the pure light of Consciousness. One knows or
experiences this as a pull to know more than a separate
sense of self, to know more than familiar experience.
And the energy that belongs to that calling is in this

instant manifesting the cosmos; a movement of energy shaping this reality from Pure Being.

I Am Now

Humans have this belief that they are not *doing* or energising what they are experiencing, but they are Awareness.

Wherever Awareness goes to, energy flows to and manifests either belief or Knowing. The cosmos as a totality remains whole in that it is a perfect reflection in this singular moment of what truly is.

Within it the dance of energy dances to the tune of Awareness not led by the power of Pure Knowing, but led by thoughts and feelings in the belief: 'I existed in the past'.

When Awareness discovers, 'I *am* Now', Now ceases to be just a word. Now is pure openness in which phenomenal forms of Awareness arise within the light of Awareness, which is self-radiating and only knowing itself, only knowing Knowing.

Day Twelve

*"Is this awakening in linear time
or is it a vertical reality
that then has appearance
in the horizontal plane?"*

Wave Upon Wave

It is a strange moment this last morning of the retreat, a strange encounter with wildly serene Reality.

Serene, in that the ground of Reality *is* serenity, like the calmness of a deep ocean. *Wildly* serene because at any moment a familiar wave could move again.

The ocean has no idea how waves keep moving to its surface, these waves of Reality called the cosmos, called the universe, called Beingness, called humanity.

"Ahhh, there is that familiar wave!" A familiar wave of thought and feeling or of a relatedness to the deep in its serenity and to the wave in its wildness. This is a constant encounter.

The light of Reality, this infinite moment Here and Now, ever present, meets its wave as if it moves in time, as if it existed yesterday and is heading towards a future. This wave that in one moment contains the serene and in the next moment the wildness of situations, mental or emotional, within oneself or apparent other selves.

Suddenly the encounter with serene Reality is wild, at times wonderfully wild, other times terribly wild in the sense of self, as Reality encounters itself in the formed levels in all its conditionality of likes and dislikes, of polarity.

Whichever way it seems, in truth this encounter with Reality is serene, the ground of it all is serenity. There is so, so much here! Human life is always in this wildness and one never knows what one will come upon.

The First Relating

The first relating in awakened-ness is in the deep, in the unfamiliar. Then that relating, whilst you have a form, moves up into the *forming*. Within this, there is a response-ability to this Knowing that is so different than the images up on this conditional level of apparent humanness.

If you don't belong to the deep, conditions will grab you and contort your perception of 'What Is'. If Awareness belongs to patterns it *must* distort and contort our perception in our relatedness.

The encounter of Reality as Awareness is utterly serene. It is the openness we experience when we truly surrender or drop in. The calling is to be true to this, within what appears to be *this* individual.

Bit-con

B reads the writing on someone's T-shirt: "Bitcoin expert...."

Bit-con expert…that fits! It is the *bits* that con
us! Images con us to believe in the image and the power
of the image.

It has to be like this for the very power of that *is*
producing everything. It is a shining of Reality,
appearing as manifestation. It is in bits; a flower, a
person, a chair, the sky, the cosmos but it is All within a
bright wholeness that is the ground of All That Is.

Seeing and Knowing

There is inherent freedom within every apparent image,
no matter what. The seer and the knower is the One
seeing and knowing. When we look at an apparent
object, the seeing of that object is the seeing of the
knowing of the seeing. It is the light of Awareness prior
to an object, which is an *appearance* of the seeing and
knowing.

Seeing and knowing is in our sensation. The hand is
actually the seeing and knowing as a hand, the foot is
the seeing and knowing as a foot, as a walk. The body is
a 'walking seeing and knowing' of the one who sees
and knows. Never does it objectify. Seeing and knowing
arises in bright-full Awareness, which returns to seeing
and knowing and even beyond the sense of 'I' - back to
the black board.

When I was in art school we used to say: "Let's get back to the black board!", like we do every night when we go to sleep.

Right now this appearance of 'somebody-ness' is arising in Awareness, the Reality that shines without beginning or end. Place your attention on the sensation in your body. Just in this 'being aware of sensation' you discover you are not 'a shape'. Your hand is not a shape, your foot is not a shape, your head is not a shape, your body is not a shape. You can literally follow the sensation into the depth, beyond sensation, directly into the Knowing-Aware-Nothing-Aware. In that moment the game is over. There is the calm of the ocean, the serene encounter with 'What Is' - Reality. And no-one is encountering it!

May it Turn to Dust

Awareness may experience the undoing of its forms as vibration, energy, thoughts and feeling colliding. The mind, so identified with naming and labelling turns to dust.

Have you ever seen dust in a stream of light? When sunlight pierces through a window or a crack and how the dust is dancing like the finest particles of gold?

Have you ever truly surrendered to a deep Knowing and experienced this within? Everything is perfectly ok, and even though all those forms have just turned to dust, all is shining in the light of opened Awareness?

A Vertical Reality

Is there anything that holds us prisoners but our lack of
being one with our Knowing? Your heart may beat and
race, adrenaline may pump though your body in facing
the imprint of a self-need and self-want. If you are not
against this because you are knowing what this
movement is, you are returned to the profundity of the
light of Reality itself. Is this not the one who is Here-
Now and never was anywhere else?

Is awakening in linear time or is it a vertical Reality that
then has appearance in the horizontal plane?

Do we speak to each other to have confirmation that we
are limited? Do we speak to each other to get what we
want and to maintain a lie? Do we relate to continue the
obsession with a conditional human experience,
affirming that we are needy and that we are lost or have
lost? Or do we speak to each other to find, not seek but
to *find* that we have already been found? for it is the
ground of 'What Is' and it is the one who is listening to
these words.

Yes, the deep is tough in a reality that is held together
through belief, but the deep is gentled when Awareness
returns this level of experience to a little bit deeper than
the familiar. Is this not going to happen at the apparent
moment of death, where absolutely nothing can be held
onto?

What is it like then to die *now*, with not one sensation,
one thought, one feeling, not one person or one
experience to be held onto? Is that not death?

What actually dies? Is it 'I' or my illusions and delusions? Is it not far more difficult to hold on to energy that is naturally moving and changing? Is it not far more difficult to hold on to all these images than to let them go? Is this not what takes place when one drops into apparent sleep?

Is this not all there really is to see and know?

Can You Stand Alone?

Here in this retreat field there is more available for the transformation, the 'beyond-formation' or the formation of the beyond in the present moment of this level of humanness. This is the wonderful capacity within two or more, who are gathered in the name of what is deeper than an ordinary limited sense of self. Is there anyone doing it other than Being-Aware-Knowing?

But even amongst this field, can you stand alone? Can you be non-relative whilst you relate to all relationships? Can you stand out without needing to stand out, stand up, stand free in the field of human relatedness *as it is,* at whatever stage of evolution it is? Can you stand free in that?

Is this not what you are called to? Realising deeper? Standing free, not *away* from anyone, but within it all?

About B

*"When I say I Am, please endeavor
not to rest your eye on the speaker.
I am speaking about this moment of One.*

*I am awake as What I Am
I am not the person on the chair,
although the self, the person
is integrated in What I Am.*

*I am landing What I Am through the heart
into the body-mind experience.
I am the bringer of the unseen
into the seen of this world.
You are the same One."*

Born in 1954 in England, B's childhood and teenage years were marked by profound mystical experiences. At age 19 he awakened in the realisation of Oneness and at 33 he opened into the Absolute. Within this unfolding he was graced with the rare and profound realisation of the Bhagavati, the divine Feminine Principle. Following realisation his known life up to that point was entirely shattered. A life of service in utter dedication to the awakening and evolution of humanity began and continues to unfold.

B offers a profoundly unique and enlightening perspective on life from the smallest matters that shape our personal lives to the biggest universal questions of human existence. His teaching and transmission is the ultimate calling to awaken as Awareness-Knowing.

With true compassion, humour and uncompromising truth, B brings the highest teaching straight to our core and into daily life. His call is to profoundly awaken whilst living in the world and his discourses cover all areas of life - relationships, sexuality, work and creativity, parenting and children, all brought to an awakening heart of Conscious Awareness.

B currently lives in New Zealand and travels extensively offering talks, seminars and residential retreats. People around the world come to B as they are waking up from the dream and conditional belief of a separate sensed self.

B is the Originator of *The Form Reality Practice*, a powerful movement practice and vehicle of awakening that is the living embodiment and transmission of realisation.

He is the Founder of She Universe, a community in New Zealand dedicated to the awakening and living of one's highest possibility of love and creativity.

The Power of Satsang

Satsang can be the most incredibly beautiful 'place' on the planet. It's not just a conversation, a movement of thought-forms but a movement of Being, together. It is a movement of the beyond.

The beyond is manifesting that communion into form and in that form there is no history, no birth date, no death date; instant Oneness, instant opening. All that we know we love in that One.

The body is not of the past. The body is the display of the field of our communion, of our being One together.

It is what we're here for. The communion and the recognition of the deep having bright Awareness, wonderful bright form, moving in the deep, moving from the deep having immediate expression with no past, no one, no separation, no other. An intimacy of profundity! We may call it God. I call it the Good with no other, no opposite.

One constant availability of the Beingness of Truth that *does* exist as 'I', *does* have a body called 'am' and that is also transcendent as 'is'. All here, moving, knowing, full of wonderful nobody-ness, full of wonderful everybody-ness, giving us deeper access into our union.

We are going into the deep through the One that we truly are even though the mind might tell us we are many. Truly there is only one and the display is many expressions of the One. It is an artistry of Love.

Profound Love, to move in, to share in, to see in, to know in and to *be* in the direct experience of and *as* that Love. It has wonderful immediate form of what that prior union is.

Be prior to all of these thoughts, all of these feelings, all of the stories, all of these notions of separation, be prior to all that! Be prior! Be prior!

*"His name was Bernie
and then it changed to B.
B really means 'being it all'.
Whoever this is, even the energy of B
is the realisation.
I am You. We are that One.
A cell has transformed into the wholeness
and lives it and there is still more."*

I Am Awareness

I am very clear that I am Awareness. Very clear that that is who is here. I am not pointing to this body. I am saying that all that is here is Awareness. Awareness is here moving in Consciousness and for us in this domain of reality, in human form.

To me we have never been apart. Never ever been apart. I know you as my own Real Self. This is not just satsang talk. This is what I am. This is also what you are.

Every day you are having darshan. Every day you are given satsang, you are given darshan even by the woman you are buying your groceries from. You look into her eyes and she is giving you darshan! You are giving her the money and you are giving her darshan. It is all darshan. It is *all* God, knowing, seeing, being, moving, manifesting and disappearing.

This is it!

It is the movement of Love. The movement of Love
without any person or self moving it and yet it moves in
self, in person and in a world.

To find out more about B Prior's
teaching and events worldwide, go to:

www.bprior.org

or contact:

B Prior Foundation
30 Teddington Rd
Governors Bay 8971

info@bernieprior.org
+64 3 3299 288

Also by B Prior:

Love Without Duality – Awakening in Intimacy

Only Love is Pouring